TOP FELLAS

THE STORY OF MELBOURNE'S SHARPIE CULT

TOP FELLAS

THE STORY OF MELBOURNE'S SHARPIE CULT

BY TADHG TAYLOR

Copyright Tadhg Taylor 2004
Third edition 2013

All rights reserved.
No parts of this book may be reproduced in any form without permission in writing from the publisher.

Published by Surefire Productions
surefireproductions@hotmail.com

Presented by
The LedaTape Organisation
www.ledatape.net

Typesetting and design by Iain McIntyre, Adele Daniele and Simon Strong.

National Library of Australia Cataloguing-in-publication entry:
Taylor, Tadhg.
Top Fellas
ISBN 978-0-9874122-7-0

1 Australia- popular culture. 2 Austalia- rock music. 3 Australia- the 1960's. 4 Australia- the 1970's. 5 Australia- youth gangs. 6 Australia- sharpies and skinheads.
I. Title.

This publication of the first edition was generously assisted by the City Of Melbourne through its Local Community History Publishing Grant Program.

CONTENTS

Author's Preface 9

Chapter 1: 1964- 1970 13

Chapter 2: 1970- 1972 41

Chapter 3:1972- 1976. 47
Lobby Loyde 73
Greg Macainsh 89

Chapter 4: 1976- 1980 91
Angry Anderson 93
Chane Chane 102
John Bow 115

Chapter 5: The Eighties . . . 119

Acknowledgements 123

A NOTE ON THE 2010 EDITION

Top Fellas was originally published in 2004 with the help of a City of Melbourne Local Community History Publishing Grant. It sold out in a few months through a handful of outlets and people have been asking me for copies ever since. That this reprint exists is down to Simon Strong 'The world's most obscure underground novelist'. He doesn't want any credit but he deserves it.

    Flicking through the book now I've got a few reservations. It's a tad overwritten and hyperbolic. The summary of UK skinheads is a bit light and my judgment of the Richard Allen books, based on memory, did Jim Moffet a disservice. He was a talented writer and his lapses should be judged in relation to the strains and demands of working in the pulp jungle. What stands up most for me about the book is the first person stories supplied by the sharpie veterans I interviewed. Meeting this lot was the highlight of the undertaking. Getting thumbs up from them on the final product was icing on the cake.

PREFACE

In my teenage years, in the mid-to-late eighties, I was a skinhead. Mention skinheads and most people think 'racist thug'. I'll deal with that falsehood in due time, suffice to say it aint necessarily so, and it certainly wasn't of my mates and I.

Skinhead weekends meant looking for parties to crash. The parties generally turned out to be duds, or the figment of somebody's imagination, or we'd get there and one of our more excitable recruits would instigate a ruckus and we'd have to split. We'd inevitably end up sitting at some boondock train station, passing around a cask of two-buck chuck and waiting for the last train into the city, or worse, the first. On sundry such occasions older blokes staggered over (they were always pretty well lubricated) and gave us an ear-bashing about how they too had been skinheads, back in the early seventies when Melbourne was wall to wall skins.

This was news to us. We were one-eyed Anglophiles, the British skins we'd seen on the telly, in magazines and on album covers were our sole inspiration. We were mere

sprouts in the early seventies, knew next to nothing about sharp's golden age, and had but vague memories of its eighties decline. What's more, we didn't really give a hoot, we couldn't see that sharpies and skinheads were in any way connected.

But somewhere along the line our interest was piqued. We came across Kevin Pappas' 1973 postcard snap of the Melbourne Sharps and it bowled us over. These were spiffy customers, decked out in the same kind of hard-mod gear that we went in for. Then we discovered the Coloured Balls 'Ballpower' album and that was that.

We were hooked, and took to grilling anyone we knew who was old enough to hip us to what this sharpie stuff was all about.

The years piled up and we grew out of the skinhead thing, but a lot of the friendships forged in those days endured. Often times when we'd get together the subject of sharpies would come up. We were still keen to know the full story and figured it was only a matter of time till someone set it down on paper. Well, come 1998 we were still waiting, and as nobody else was stepping up to bat, I decided to have a bash myself.

Take a look at any book about Australian pop-culture in the sixties and seventies. I'll lay you ten to one there'll be nothing in there about the nigh on two decade reign of the sharpie cult. Most of these books are written by academics who invariably focus on the hippy/student-protest movement, because that's where they were at in their youth. Sharpies are ignored or written off as naught but a bunch of louts, unworthy of serious attention. It all boils down to ignorance and snobbery.

I'm not an academic, so if you're after a dry-as-dust university tome, you've come to the wrong shop. My main aim in writing this book was to sketch a picture of the sharpie era that was as faithful as possible to the recollections of the ex-sharps who so graciously shared their time and tales with me. I found them a sterling bunch and hope I've done them justice.

Some may feel the book is biased towards Melbourne. Fair enough. For my money, the bias is just. Perth/Sydney/Adelaide sharps were no joke, but Melbourne was the homeland, the holy city.

When you're dealing with a movement that spanned almost two decades and went through considerable stylistic changes questions of ownership are bound to arise. Each generation that adopted the sharpie title saw themselves as the genuine article and those that followed as imposters, defiling the name. To ensure a 20/20 Panavision picture of the cult, I've taken the stance that the sharpie name belongs to all that used it, from first to last. Set side by side a sharpie of the sixties and a sharpie of the eighties may, on the surface, bear little resemblance, but there was a definite kinship in attitudes and aesthetics.

Mass-pop movements like sharpie are a microcosm of society at large. The sharp ranks were made up of individuals with a myriad of opinions, beliefs and motivations. There is no definitive account of what it meant to be a sharpie, rather there are threads that link the lives of those that identified themselves with the cult, threads that enable us to paint a general picture of the sharp experience. Some sharps were sweeties, others were dastards, a few were downright fit for the nut-hutch. Most were just kids, regular kids looking for adventure. This is their story.

...there is not one root to juvenile delinquency, but two. For all the talk of broken homes, sub marginal housing, overcrowding in schools and cultural starvation, the other root is more alive and one kills it at ones peril. It is the root for which our tongues once found the older words of courage, loyalty, honor and the urge for adventure.

Norman Mailer 1964

1

1964 - 70

"And now, from the angry ashes of the '56 rocker, our garden city Melbourne is seeing a new form of lout arise..."
Oz, October 1966.

"We're in revolt against the femininity of long hair and sissy clothes."
Denis, 17 year old sharpie, 1966.

First off there was mods and rockers. In the 1950s and 60s Australia vigorously courted potential immigrants from England with advertising campaigns that promised a sunny, egalitarian Shangrila, a land of golden opportunity. Thousands bought it hook, line and boat ticket. A lot of them ended up in Adelaide.

In the early sixties the big thing with up-to-the-minute British teenagers was 'mod' and Adelaide's migrant population had a large share of mods in its composition.

Randy
"I came to Adelaide from England in 1959. I became a mod when I was in high school. Mod happened in a big way in Adelaide, there were even a lot of scooter gangs which wasn't really the case anywhere else in the country, except maybe Brisbane. At school I'd say in a class of thirty about twenty-five would've been British, working class, from the North and Midlands. Places like Elizabeth and the Adelaide Hills were full of English immigrants. To come

from those harsh industrial cities to Adelaide, which really was beautiful then, was amazing for them. Every three weeks a new boatload of immigrants would arrive and the kids would tell us about the latest fashions and bands, consequently we were never that far behind what was happening in England."

The original mods of late fifties London where jazz loving dandies with a taste for Continental style. By the early sixties mod had caught on nation wide but in a form more accessible to the average teen. Rhythm and blues, scooters and amphetamines were the order of the day. The look remained clean-cut European cool. The mod aesthetes of the fifties had small use for gang-scraps and rough-housing. But by the early sixties the mod ranks swelled with lively lads who liked nothing better than a mash up, and thanks to a series of bank holiday skirmishes with rocker gangs, 'mod' became tabloid speak for hooliganism incarnate. At the same time the tag caught on with the general public and was being hung willy-nilly on every new pop combo and fashion fad that came down the pike. This hijacking of the mod name was viewed with horror by the cult's originals, for whom seaside riots and pop groups were equally anathema.

British mod kids that quit Adelaide for Melbourne were a key influence on the birth of sharp. Melbourne in 1963 was still rocker country, but things were changing. In their day the rocker mobs reigned supreme, but that's somebody else's book. Suffice to say, by '64 they were in decline. The mod aesthetic was catching on.

Every street gang has its junior recruits. Some of them are hip beyond their years and their age is irrelevant. Some have older brothers with big reputations and demand respect by proxy. Others act as whipping boys and mascots, there to take the older boys' shit and exhibit awe at their derring-do. In the course of time these kids climb up the hierarchy and when the older boys move on, they take over the whole operation. In '64 the younger element of the rocker scene set forth in a new direction, inspired by the neat streamlined look of mod. The older blokes were too set in their ways to follow suit. The '64 Rocker' was born.

Peter
"It was the end of the rocker days, we'd wear a black cardigan with a red shirt, or vice versa, with pants so tight you could barely get them on. Then when I was about sixteen, it all changed."

Dennis
"It started in the inner city suburbs, Collingwood, Richmond. At first we called ourselves '64 Rockers, to distinguish us from the '56 rockers, your Elvis/bodgie type. Anything they wore we'd wear the opposite. They wore peg-pants so we wore flares, that kind of thing. There was a lot of emphasis on clothes because of the mod thing in England. We were work-

ing class guys dressing up, we didn't have much money but at least we looked like we did. The point was to always look sharp, that's why people started calling us sharpies, but we never called ourselves that, you were just one of the fellas or not one of the fellas."

Robert
"I was in with the Newport boys, we'd attend local dances and generally cause havoc. We'd go to Moonee Ponds Town Hall to see people like Merv Benton, Johnny Lyle and Johnny Chester. We dressed smart, overcoats and pointed toe shoes. We'd hang around a jazz club in Newport called 'Dido', just to pick fights and hang shit on the jazzers."

So then: the '64 rocker was re-christened the sharpie. And away we go.

Hair was short back n' sides, usually parted, cut every two weeks. But then, plant your arse in a barber's chair in the mid-sixties and you had little chance of leaving with anything but a short back n' sides. It was the only dish on the menu.

The threads were swank but not foppish- dapper tough guy, sharp! Besides mod the main influence was a certain kind of migrant Italian man, denizen of inner-city coffee bars, always togged just so, spiffed but macho. Sharps were nuts for Italian style and the cult was always strongest in migrant heavy neighbourhoods, where the tailors and shoe shops they favoured were located.

You got your trousers, shirts, suits and shoes made to order, partly because you couldn't get the sharp style off the rack and partly for the thrill of one-upmanship. An up-to-date wardrobe separated the aces from the offal. If you wanted to be in the swim your threads had to make the grade, if they didn't you weren't even on the radar screen.

At first slightly flared trousers were the go, but they were soon succeeded by 'Flags', 22 inch bottoms, usually pinstripe, herring-bone or Prince of Wales check, in various hues of brown or grey. Some opted for turned up bottoms, dropping pennies in the cuffs to keep the crease knife-edge sharp.

At the height of the flag craze Camberwell's 'Morris the Tailor' had a window sign boasting he could whip up a pair in half an hour.

The basic cut of flags rarely differed but you'd strut your individuality in finicky little ways, pocket design for instance was a field of raging competition. Number of pockets, placement of pockets, shape of pocket flaps, the possibilities were endless, the rivalry intense. For my money the high-water mark of flag pocket design would have to be the ciggy pack pocket half way down the side of your leg with a V shaped button down flap. To the kid who first came up with that corker, I dip my lid.

Levi's and Lee jeans hit Melbourne around this time and made a big splash with the sharps. Some favoured Lee and others Levi's, at the end of the day I'd say it was a dead heat. Your best bet for scoring a pair was Louis Epstein's in the city, but you had to be on the ball because kids were trooping in from all over to get them. Up till then sharps had made do with denim overalls, worn under jumpers to hide the braces, but they were pushed aside quick smart when the real thing came along. Problem was the real thing set you back around five pounds, a week's wages for most sharps.

If you were going to a dance you'd don the nattiest threads on your peg, which generally meant a suit. Sharpie suits were usually dark conservative colours, pinstripe, herringbone or tonik (a fabric that's predominantly one colour but shimmers with another). Jackets were Italian single-breasted three button, or double breasted neo-thirties style, usually worn over a short sleeved Ban-lon/Crest-knit buttoned up to the neck, or a shirt buttoned likewise a la Billy Thorpe. Trousers were, of course, flag style. A tie (say, a thin square ended number) together with a tie pin and cuff links was just the shot for added swank.

Ban-lon/Crest-knit tops were short sleeved tennis shirts in the Lacoste/Ralph Lauren style. They were generally three-button, but you

could also get them with buttons all down the front. Maroon, cream and green were the poll-topping colours, and they often had contrasting stripes and piping. The Ban-lon/Crest-knit was one of the corner stones of the sharp rig-out, in vogue from the opening kick-off to the final curtain.

Everybody had a trench coat, single-breasted, white was popular, no belt. Woollen overcoats, often called boxer or bokka coats, were equally big, three-quarter length, checked, brown or charcoal grey.

Porkpie hats were popular, chocolate brown, black, hounds-tooth, generally Dobb's brand, as later worn by de Niro in 'Mean Streets'. Sticky fingered sharps nicked them from tram depot lockers.

Dennis

"I was 14 and so were most of my mates, 14 year old kids getting around in porkpie hats, well, people are gonna look at you, and when they did it was a good excuse to start a fight."

There were about ten shoemaker's frequented by sharps, but four of them had the others beat hands down- Kosmano's in Collingwood, Mediterranean in Kensington, and Acropolis and Venus in Richmond. Those names should clue you to the fact that the market was sewn up cold by Southern European gents.

In 1964 'Points' were the shoes of choice: pointy toed, suede or two-tone, slip-on or lace-up, sometimes flat soled but usually Cuban heeled, definitely a hangover from the rocker days. Points were soon thrown over in favour of 'Chisels', kind of like Points with the tips chopped off. Again the basic design was flat-soled or Cuban heeled, slip-on or lace-up. That was your foundation, the trimmings were up to you. You could get them with a brogue or baskct weave pattern, in blue suede, ox-blood, two-tone brown and white or black and white, patent leather or, if you really wanted to knock 'em cock-eyed, alligator skin!

If you were strapped for cash you could get away with buying your shoes off the shelf, but if you wanted to run with the top-liners you got them handmade. It was a point of pride.

In summer many ditched their chisels for sandals, not exactly A1 protection for your trotters should a blue occur, and they were hardly few and far between!

V neck jumpers were popular, but the big thing was cardigans, sharps dug their cardies something fierce. Cable-knit, mostly maroon but also cream, green, and blue. Worn with a Ban-lon/Crest-knit (often in a matching colour) or button-down shirt- plain or checked.

Graham
"They all looked the same and they looked bloody formidable... in their fine knits."

Some dedicated swells took to carrying fob watches and brollies. The latter lent you an air of city-gent polish and if the tip was sharpened they made a top notch weapon to boot. Many an unlucky citizen copped a brolly coronation from a sharpie hanging out of a passing train.

Most sharps had a few tats. Nowadays all kinds of mild mannered blokes get tattooed and nobody looks askance at them, but back in the sixties and seventies they still marked you as a tough guy, so a 15 or 16 year old kid already covered in them looked pretty full-on. All the golden oldies got a look in: skull and crossbones, hearts and daggers, scrolls with loved ones' names on them, 'Death Before Dishonour'. There weren't many tattooists around back then, Dickie Reynolds in Flinders Street, Danny Robinson in Williamstown, Tex in Lonsdale street. Number one with the sharps was a bloke named Alfie, who operated out of his backyard in Collingwood. Sharps came from all over Melbourne to visit Alfie, taking care to dodge the Collingwood Boys, who were usually killing time nearby in a joint called 'Half-moon Hamburgers'.

Sharpies had their own way of walking: shoulders back, wrists bent up, poker stiff, a 'cross me at your peril' strut. Throw in some spitting and fingernail biting and you cut a very lairy dash indeed.

Sharp girls were known as sharpie 'brush', which sounds a bit unflattering but is really just immemorial Aussie slang for teenage girls. Sharp girls thumbed their noses at the prevailing trends in women's fashion, all the Mary Quant dolly-bird gear, favouring crisp classic simplicity.

Dale
"There was full employment then, you could leave school and virtually get a job the next day, which is what I did. I left school at fifteen and got a job, which got me into being a sharpie girl because I could afford to buy clothes and go to dances. There were tailors in Richmond who'd make your trousers- I had a grey pinstripe pair. The first jeans I bought I had to get in the Menswear department at Myers. Sharpie girls wore round-necked dresses, sort of woollen material, short sleeved. At the time it was all short skirts but we wore knee-length pleated Sun-Ray skirts, pale pinks and blues, darker colours for winter, very straight, sophisticated."

Hair was short of course, varying in length from a Mia farrow to a Cilla Black. Twin sets were popular (short sleeved round-neck jumpers worn under matching cardigans) as were pearl earrings and necklaces. Sharpettes shared the boys' taste for trench coats, overcoats, sandals and handmade shoes. Girls' shoes were patterned after the boys' styles, but with very flat heels.

Pin-stripe suits, porkpie hats, woollen over-coats, two-tone Cuban heeled shoes- a lot of sharpie gear suggested a taste for the style of the 1920's and 30's, and more specifically the style of 1920's/30's gangster movies, a world very much in step with the sharpies' dapper tough-guy ideal. A great deal of the fashion and design of the sixties echoed that of the twenties and thirties, a trend that peaked with the release of the film 'Bonnie and Clyde'. This is not to say that every rank and file sharp in the street was self consciously harking back to the past, most were just keeping in step with their mates, but it's fair to say that somewhere along the line the influence was absorbed. One explanation is that the sharps were plagiarising the styles displayed by the elder statesmen of the sly-grogs and boxing gyms where they tended to congregate, blokes who'd remained faithful to the styles of their youth.

There were definite shades of the 'Larrikin' in the sharps' get-up and roaring-boy antics. Larrikins were very much the sharpies of their day- the last decades of the nineteenth century. They lurked nefarious around the dancing saloons, illegal drinking houses and boxing joints (not to mention the street corners and shadowy doorways) of slum Melbourne. They ran in mobs, or 'pushes', and dressed with great flair, black slouch hats, collarless shirts, velvet collared jackets, red neckerchiefs and, here's the clincher, bell-bottom trousers and tailor-made boots with outlandishly high heels and ornate detailing!

There was a definite hierarchy in the sharpie world. The scene's killer-elite were known as 'Top Fellas'. To be a Top Fella you had to be handy in a blue, hell on the dance floor, cocksure with the brush, and dapper as all get out. Known, connected and respected- a sharpie's sharpie. Then there were the 'Older Fellas' the battle-hardened sharp originals, in their early twenties and revered by all. A 'Gunny', as the name implies, was a bloke whose pocket bulged with a hidden persuader, a gun-man. You didn't need to be a sharp to be known as a Gunny, the name was also given to any crim or docker that carried a pistol, but there were a number of Gunnies in the sharp scene, particularly in the inner-city squads. A 'Knockabout' was someone who was in the fold, but not the vanguard, an everyman. An 'Apprentice' was a hanger-on, a bloke that just couldn't make the grade, or alternately just a novice, yet to prove his mettle. The lowest of the low were called 'Chats'. First World War Diggers referred to the lice that plagued the trenches as chats. In sharp lingo it meant pariah, in for a hiding. It's not like these were permanently set ranks, or that blokes went around skiting about being 'Top Fellas' or cringing because they were 'Apprentices', but these were the terms used when someone's clout, or lack thereof, was discussed.

By 1966 sharpie style had swamped the suburbs and every area of Melbourne boasted a sharp crew or three. Some were modest, undersized mobs, content to stay put in their territory, slug it out with neighbouring teams and lord it over the local teenage populace. Others were veritable armies, journeying far and wide on search and destroy missions. It wasn't all spiffy strides.

Martin.
"A lot of blokes dressed real fancy, suits with short European jackets and velvet collars, but they weren't mods and they were rough as guts working class."

Peter.
"We'd rather have a fight than a feed."

In '66 the papers were full of reports of pitched battles between sharpies and mods, most of which were more than somewhat wide of the truth. There were differences and sometimes conflict between the two groups, but the real action was elsewhere-sharp v rockers, sharp v surfies, and most commonly sharp v sharp, that is neighbourhood against neighbourhood.

Defining what the word 'mod' meant in sixties Melbourne, is a tall order indeed. When the newsmen referred to mods, they meant any youngster who wore colourful duds and sported a Beatle do, a misnomer that was greatly resented by the scores of Melbourne kids that lived by the original mod ethos.

Peter M.
"In 1966/67 when I was about 15 I became a mod. Being a mod was about sartorial elegance, you dressed in a way you believed was super-smart and particularly noticeable. That didn't mean you went around in outlandish clothes, you just needed to look like you were paying a lot of attention, not just to your appearance but to everything that was going on. Sharp Italian suits, loafers, short hair-that was the quintessential mod look, which peaked in England around 1964/65. For some reason, and I can only put it down to the tyranny of distance, that look lingered in Australia for some years, and that's how the people I mixed with dressed. But at the same time the average Australian's idea of mod was long hair and outlandish clothes, while the people who dressed in the original mod style were called stylists."

The mod-purists/stylists listened to soul and rhythm n' blues, and followed local groups like the Chelsea Set and the Purple Hearts (featuring Lobby Loyde), groups that played R&B with a bit of Who style crash-bang-wallop. Their home base was the Thumpin' Tum in Little Latrobe Street, Melbourne's most up-to-the-minute dance, a weird world of flashing po-

lice lights, Victorian era prints and umbrellas, dozens of upside down umbrellas covering every inch of the roof.

The term 'stylist' was coined in England. The mod elite adopted the label to distinguish themselves from the Johnny-come-lately rocker battling variant. Melbourne's sharps and mod-purists/stylists weren't exactly brothers in arms, but they managed to co-exist without too much friction. Sharp was really just a knockabout version of English mod and by 67/68 there were quite a few ex-sharps in the stylist camp. As the stylist handle caught on it too lost its original meaning and was used to describe any kid in a Myers 'In-Gear' ensemble. Things got doubly confusing as the original stylists/mod-purists drifted away from Italian suiting and into the more exotic togs of the psychedelic era. Mods, stylists, long-hairs, whatever-the-hells, if they had long hair and effeminate clothes sharps didn't like them, and many weren't above expressing their distaste with a smack in the mouth. The fact that sharps were invariably on the dog-list at mod/long-hair dances didn't exactly help foster good relations between the two sides. Nor did the media. By beating up a few

mod/sharp blues into a full-scale gang war, the papers threw bucket loads of fat into the fire. But at the end of the day belting long-hairs was just a nasty lark, there was no war. It takes two to tangle and most of Melbourne's mods/long-hairs just weren't interested.

Rockers loved a battle but alas by the time sharpies took the stage the rocker ranks were somewhat anorexic. Nonetheless they definitely kept their end up and rocker/sharp biff-sessions were often photo finishes.

Surfies were more like it. There were lots of them, they hated sharps and they were far more war-like than you might think.

But the real hell for leather brawling was sharp v sharp.

Arthur
"I became a sharp when I was about 14, this was 64/65. We had about fifty lads in our gang, mostly from Oakleigh, a few from Springvale and Clayton, and two from Mordiallic- Doberman and Lurch, awesome reputations. The prominent gangs were Prahran, St Kilda, Collingwood, Port Melbourne, Broadmeadows, they were very fashionable and

had big reputations. They'd come down wanting to fight the Oakleigh boys, and we'd oblige them.

One of our boys, Ralphy, had a run in with an ex-girlfriend who was going with one of the Collingwood boys, a lad called Dinger Bell. We were in our local haunt one night, a pub called the Junction, more commonly known as the Blood-House, and these Collingwood boys came in looking for Ralphy. There was only a few of us, myself, Johnny Flappers, and a lad called the Beast, who was a legendary king-hit merchant. They pushed us a little too far. We were out numbered and a bit scared so we went on the attack, just to cover ourselves. We went into them with everything in the shop, it spilled onto the footpath, and they bolted off under a barrage of chairs, crying 'We'll be back'. A few weeks later we're down the pub and they're back, over sixty of them. We jumped the bar, ran into the toilets, I spent half the night hiding under a car, Collingwood boys all around. We had a lot of run-ins with them after that, shotguns were pulled, a car was torched, but that was the only time they got the upperhand."

Ken
"I was from Sandringham, all up there was about thirty kids in our gang. Collingwood and St Kilda were the big gangs, very tough. Occasionally they'd come to Sandringham, looking for fights. The St Kilda boys, 'St Kilda Saints and Sinners' they were called, came down to a dance at the Mentone LifeSaving Club one night, about eighty of them, massive blue, guys getting pushed off the balcony."

Peter
"I was from Williamstown, we didn't like Altona or Newport, we hung around with the Fawkner/Brunswick guys and had a slight affiliation with the Sunshine boys. Once we got cars you'd have twenty car loads of us drive to a dance, say Stonehenge in Beaumaris. One guy would pay to get in, open up the back doors, and we'd all pile in and fix 'em up. The biggest fight I ever saw was at the Myer Music Bowl, about two thousand sharps, East meets West, and it was on. Preston was probably the biggest gang in Melbourne, their leader was a guy called Pappas. In Sunshine it was a bloke called Alex, had about five brothers, Maltese origin. He was almighty, if he looked at you you'd look away. The story goes that this guy called Ryan, a gangster from North Melbourne, came looking for him, had a big black guy with him. Ryan pulled a gun on him and that was the end of Alex, he's still alive but he disappeared for a long time after that."

Most ex-sharps will tell you that they had a code of conduct. If you stuck to the code you were said to have 'good form'.

If you had a beef with someone you'd settle the matter with a fair-square one-out fistfight. To call in the cavalry and bash him five-on-one was considered very shabby form.

You didn't use weapons in a one-out blue. Toting a weapon marked you as gutless. Gang-warring was a little different. Most did stick to fist-fighting, but there were times when you needed that something extra just to even up the odds. A handful of heavy-duty customers carried knives or guns, but most made do with something from the shed- hammers, crowbars etc. If you were caught unawares and outnumbered by a rival team, a fence post made for a nifty equaliser. Plant a kick at their lowest point and they came off quick as a wink.

Arthur
"One night we went to a party to stitch up the Jordanville boys. Someone tipped off the police that we were coming and they were there when we pulled up. They lined us up, searched the cars and found a metre long steel Vic-Rail spanner. I'd put it in the car and I owned up to it. I was charged with larceny and having an offensive weapon. As I'd been such a mischief-maker I ended up getting 12 months in the Bayswater youth training centre. It was very much an attempt to thin out the ranks, we already had one of the gang up there and a couple in the Yogs,

the Pentridge young offenders unit."

Peter
"There was a code, we were respectful of say, a husband and wife out with their kids, the shits these days they don't care. I never used weapons, no knives, nothing. I never believed in kicking people, but after receiving a particularly vicious beating I thought, it's do or die. I still never gave anyone a real kicking but I did get called the Williamstown City Stomper...I stomped on them."

If a crew caught up with an enemy when he was all by his lonesome, or out with a girlfriend, they'd most likely let him walk on by. To give him a trouncing in such a situation would be a low-blow unworthy of a class-mob. Of course the same mob, on another night, with a bit of grog under their belts, might not be feeling quite so classy.

If a lone sharp was copping a hiding from a bunch of rockers or surfies you were duty bound to wade in and lend a fist. In another time and place he might be your enemy, but that didn't matter. He was still one of the fellas.

Sharps fought sharps but there was rarely any deep-felt enmity involved. For most it was just an exciting diversion. There were a few bad eggs, blokes that were simply out to maim and didn't know honour from a hole in the ground, but most kept things relatively gentlemanlike. The point of sharp gang clashes wasn't to

wipe out your opponents and end the war. You wanted to wreck them, but not for keeps. It was more sporting, gladiatorial. You fought for the rush and to earn a rep, and no matter who came off best you'd meet again soon for a rematch.

Arthur
"There was always a bit of tension in the shoe shop."

Sharps would travel from far-off suburbs to visit Venus, Acropolis et al, and there was always the risk of ambush by local gangs. But though the journey to the shops was fraught with danger, the shops themselves were Switzerland. There was a tacit agreement among the gangs that all grudges should be checked at the door. There was no brawling in the shoe shop. Greasies were thrown, but no punches.

To pay such loving attention to the minutiae of your dress and then risk it all in backstreet punch-ons might seem a little non compis mentis, but it was simply a matter of devotion to the cause. A lot of sharps were apprentices in mucky, hands-on trades, but would still front up to work decked out in flags, chisels,

the whole shootin' match. Being a sharpie meant you dressed right 365. Anything less would be half-stepping and half-stepping doesn't get it done.

Rival gangs weren't the only callers to contend with, the police were a constant threat as well. A certain mob of city coppers prowled the suburbs in their Studdebaker Hawks, keeping an eye on the natives. Their objective was to stamp out the gangs, and by all accounts they weren't averse to pouring on the rough stuff to get a result.

Arthur
"In the fifties you had the Bodgie Squad and these guys were a similar thing. They'd come down to Oakleigh with their porkpie hats on and it was backs against the wall, on your toes and a punch in the gut. If they got you on your own they'd beat the crap out of you no ifs or buts. They'd get you down the station and try and provoke you. They'd give you a right whack and you just had to take it."

Only a reckless few fought back, to do so would've most likely meant a fearful hiding and a long stretch in a boys' home. Which is not to say everyone just turned the other cheek and let bygones be bygones. Many took their bruises when they had to and kicked back when the odds were more favourable. Occasionally one of the gang-busters found himself in the wrong place at the wrong time and got his spuds cooked but good.

I've heard talk of a band of undercover cops called the Silent Six who were roundly hated in sharp circles. Supposedly their brief was to break up any group of teenagers they found loitering in the city. Their tactics are said to have included dishing out thirty pound fines for the use of salty language, a handsome ransom in the sixties, particularly to teenage apprentices with a mania for tailored plumage.

Another method the cops are supposed to have used to rid the city of trouble making mobs was to march them down to Flinders Street Station and press gang them onto trains bound for the suburbs. Not necessarily the suburbs they hailed from, they just stuck them on the first train that pulled in!

I've also heard talk of a 'long-hair' squad, cops with pop-star tresses, dolled up in full flower-power regalia, who hung around the city waiting for sharpies to attack them. That's what I've been told, so that's what I'm telling you, but I wouldn't bet my shirt on its veracity.

The bottom-line is that the police did not love the sharpies very much and troubled their tracks something chronic. Sometimes they'd manhandle them. Dishing out this kind of 'summary justice' was normal procedure in the sixties, when a rap on the knuckles or clout on the ear were considered acceptable ways of licking young men into shape.

It's fair to say that most people will break the law at some point in their teenage years. Obviously I don't mean full-tilt crime, like robbing banks and what have you, I'm talking about vandalism, shoplifting, borrowing unattended automobiles, all that bees-wax. These are foolish irresponsible acts, to that verdict there is no appeal, but what are teenagers for if not to do foolish irresponsible things? Most grow out of it. Most but not all. The summit of most sharpies' criminal careers was knocking a copper's hat off at the Melbourne show, but for others the sharp life was the first step down the dead-end of crime and violence.

Dennis

"A lot of my immediate friends had been in boys homes, Turana, Morning Star, some just because they came from broken homes, little guys with chips on their shoulders. A lot got arrested for stupid stuff, offensive behaviour, shop-lifting when they were broke after spending all their money on clothes. I got out of it and for the next ten years I'd read about people I'd known doing bank robberies and other heavy things. One of them, Michael Ebert was shot dead in Carlton in 1980. He'd been running some massage parlours and had obviously stepped on somebody's toes. His dying words, as reported by the 'Truth', were 'You'll

die for this'. **He was a really nice guy but schizophrenic for sure, after a few beers he was like Joe Pesci in Goodfellas."**

Michael Ebert gets a brief mention in Chopper Read's first book 'From the Inside'. Chopper was a sharp himself, but we'll get into that a little further down the road. A man that Read seems to have great respect for is Ray 'Chuck' Bennet, the brains behind the 'Great Bookie Robbery' of 1976, a legendary heist that netted Bennet and his crew between 1.4 and 12 million dollars. The exact sum is unknown on account of the bookies being understandably cagey about the revealing the size of their kitty. Bennet was a master of his trade, responsible for a string of big money armed robberies. His brilliant career came to an end when he was shot dead in the Melbourne Magistrates Court in 1979. His death was allegedly a blood for blood killing, set up by his lifelong foe Brian Kane to avenge the death of his brother Les. In his teens Bennet was apparently a sharpie, and if the oft-printed mug-shot of him, clad in a dilly of a checked overcoat, is anything to go by, I'd say he remained an uncommonly well-clad bloke till his dying day.

Peter David McEvoy, associate of the notorious Allen/Pettingill clan is also said to have been a sharp.

Fact is these blokes are just the tip of the iceberg. Delve into the youth of any Aussie bad-man that grew up in the sixties or seventies and there's a good chance you'll find he rose from the ranks of a sharpie crew.

A number of boxers rose from those ranks as well. Being such a scrap-happy bunch it was only natural that a lot of sharps would enter the rope-arena. Inner city gyms like Leo Berry's in Richmond were always full of sharps and transformed a lot of sharpie street fighters into first-rate pugilists. These blokes were the absolute upper-strata of sharp, older fellas and real toughies, but slick with it. They made a fair wage fighting so they were always silked to the bone in the sharpest of sharp threads. In the eyes of the young sharpie multitude these guys were what it was all about, the sharpie ideal made flesh. One-time Commonwealth Featherweight Champ Bobby Dunn, who sadly passed away in 1998, was one such sharp turned fighter.

Dale
"Bobby Dunn ended up teaching dancing in Bundoora, because he was a boxer he was great on his feet. I was lucky enough to dance with him and it was like dancing with Fred Astaire. He still wore flag pants and had the hair, he was wonderful."

Sharps took their dancing very seriously. An A-grade dancer enjoyed a standing comparable to that of an A-grade fighter. If you were both you had it made in the shade.

Peter
"We all loved to dance, there was no wallflower stuff, you'd dance on your own, you were frightened of no-one."

Every youth cult creates its own dances, sharpies came up with two, the Break and the Sharpie Rock. The Rock was a bit of a throwback to the rock n' roll dances of the fifties. You could dance it alone or with a partner and sometimes one bloke would dance with two girls. The bloke would twirl the girl around and often in doing so the girl's skirt would blow up, revealing her stockings and suspenders, a spectacle that the fellas didn't despise one jot.

The Break, often referred to as the Sharpie Shuffle by people outside the scene, was a kind of line dance. There were lots of variations on the moves performed, but the chief thing was to line everyone up shoulder to shoulder, all dancing in unison. If every-bod was on the beat it looked mighty impressive.

Dale
"Back then Melbourne was buzzing, there were dances everywhere, every second warehouse in the city was a dancehall. We'd go to 'That's Life' on Chapel street, Windsor, 'The White Elephant' at Broadmeadows town hall, 'Tenth Avenue' in the city,

and always to 'The Bowl' on Fridays."

Located near Flinders Street Station, beneath a bowling alley at 21 Degreaves Street, the Bowl was Melbourne's foremost sharpie haunt. The Bowl offered big name bands and a DJ spinning the kind of records sharps favoured. Sharpies liked American soul and British beat sounds, music of the r n' b genus, music that led to crowded dance-floors. Big-timers such as The Easybeats, Normie Rowe, The Masters Apprentices, Max Merritt and the Meteors, Billy Thorpe and Ronnie Burns (who according to one source had his nose broken by a sharpie 'fan') were doing the circuit at the time, and were all well liked by the sharp crowd. Lesser known groups such as The Browns, led by legendary guitarman Les Stacpool, were also popular. Singer John 'Swanee' Swan told me that for sheer voluminous bloodshed, Browns' gigs took the biscuit hands down.

Dale
"The stylists got more into Sergeant Pepper and all that gear, I was never big on that, I would say sharpies liked more the Motown music, the Stones, the Animals, that's what they played at the Bowl, because it was dance music, and that's basically what we were there for."

The Bowl opened in late '64 and was originally a mod dance, but by mid '65 the sharps were well and truly in residence. Like all the dancehalls the Bowl was an all-ages, teetotal affair, but there was always alcohol in the air as most of the clientele kicked off the evening with a spot of unlawful thirst quenching at Young and Jackson's.

Dale
"Friday night after The Bowl shut there would inevitably be a blue. It sounds horrible to say but it was kind of like your weekend wasn't anything until that happened."

The Bowl was a rough and rowdy joint. Brawls were common. But the atmosphere was more extrovert than threatening, the bottom line was fun, and if you got too unruly you'd have to tangle with the bouncer, Stretch, a veteran sharp street-fighter/pugilist of colossal repute.

A rocker dance was held every Friday night above Flinders Street train station in the Vic Rail ballroom, mere spitting distance from the Bowl, so if you grew tired of rug-ripping and felt like handing out some bloodshed you need only step outside. The two teams would lock horns every Friday at closing time and the proceedings could get pretty ferocious. One ex-sharp told me of a night he was chased by a mob of rockers wielding iron baling-hooks that they'd liberated from the rail yards.

The Circle Ballroom in High Street Preston was another popular sharpie hang-out. Sunday nights at the Circle the whole scene came together, giving the youngsters a chance to rub shoulders with the older fellas. The Circle was one of the few dances the older sharps frequented, mostly they were to be found in pubs, pool-halls or

at the track. Some of the older blokes were clothes conscious in the extreme, setting the pace for the lower orders. Others no longer gave two shits and dressed decidedly un-sharp. Nobody was going to scold them for it. In general a laissez fair attitude to matters of dress was unacceptable, but rank had its privileges. Quite a few of them had done time and some carried guns. It didn't pay to piss them off.

In the mid-to-late sixties most dances catered to long-hairs, sharps were generally barred for fear they'd demolish the joint. When they did manage to get in they were still on the outer, with most of the crowd eye-balling them with suspicion. In September '66 a woman named Marge Marsh, whose daughter Suzanne was a sharp, took it upon herself to redress the situation.

Suzanne
"My mother was very understanding of the trials of being a teenager and used to listen to the woes of our little group. She decide to inquire about hiring a hall strictly for sharps, so they'd have a place to go, to keep them off the streets. She hired a hall in Elwood and held a number

of dances there. She also hired bouncers in case of trouble, and got a lot of discount advertising on the radio."

The dance was christened 'The Tavern' and opening night went off aces, with a turn out of nigh on five hundred sharps and no hint of trouble. But a few weeks later some of the peppier element of the mod scene turned up intent on tearing the place down. The sharps could hardly cry foul, their track record vis-à-vis mod dances wasn't exactly snow white, but unfortunately the confrontation made the papers and the hall's owner, who hadn't reckoned on his property being used as a gangland battlefield, tore up Marge's lease. The Tavern shifted from venue to venue, but the mods kept coming and the fur kept flying, for a while anyway. Eventually both sides grew tired of the fighting and a truce was called. Consequently the Tavern became an integrated sharp/mod affair with no trouble to speak of for the rest of its six-month lifespan.

In late '66 a dance called The Catcher opened, a momentous occasion for Melbourne's teenage populace. Up till then all dances had closed at midnight, but the Catcher stayed open well into the wee small hours. The Catcher was really geared towards the long-hair crowd, but sharps were generally allowed in and many made it their regular weekend habitat. Before the Catcher opened the only joints still going after night's high noon were the 'sly-grogs'.

For many moons Australian drinkers suffered under laws that required pubs to close by 6pm on weekdays and prohibited them from opening on Sundays. These were the days of the 'six o' clock swill', when the call for last orders signalled the beginning of a tap-draining beer bacchanal.

During this time the sly-grogs thrived. The sly-grogs were pubs or private houses where the booze flowed at all hours, regardless of the law- on the sly as it were. Sharpies were all deep drinkers. Some had a taste for rebel pharmaceuticals, Purple Hearts and the like, but they were a tiny minority, booze was the poison of choice. Most sharps were too young to pass muster at pubs, so the sly-grogs were a godsend.

Arthur
"The main mission was drinking. **Sundays we'd do the rounds of the sly-grogs, Dickie Reirdon's in Richmond, one near Moorabin Airport, one in Clarendon Street South Melbourne, a private house in Murrumbeena. Just drop the password and away you go."**

Robert
"**Drink of the day was Barossa Pearl and Crème de Menth. If you were underage you'd get it from a sly-grog, you'd ring from a nearby phone box and collect it from the side entrance, the pub would be all in darkness."**

Peter
"When I was sixteen I was hanging around with a guy called Big John, who was about twenty nine, a big age difference. He took us to a place in Collingwood called The Blue Angel Café. I'll never forget it, it was like a speak-easy. There was a peephole in the door, a three-piece combo, and they were selling claret in Coke bottles. It got raided and it was just like the movies, red lights flashing, everybody running. Massive coppers, never seen coppers that big. This was before night clubs, everything closed at ten. Usually when we went to a dance we'd buy some beer and hide the bottles up a drainpipe, they stayed cool up there. Of course some bastard would usually come and pinch them."

Sharpie was as much a middle class phenomenon as it was working class, but it was born in the working class inner-city, and it's fair to say its mindset was working class- larrikin. The average sharp girl worked in an office and the blokes were usually apprentices or shop assistants, a lot of them in the rag trade. But for most work was but a means to an end, it kept their pockets lined, the weekend was what really mattered.

During the week most sharps stayed in their neighbourhoods, meeting up

with their mates after work. Most gangs had a coffee bar/hamburger joint that served as a meeting place cum base of operations. But on Saturday arvo the whole sharp world would be at large in the city. There were always scraps, but it wasn't all hate and war, there was a lot of brotherhood as well. The city was the place where everyone came together and first port-of-call was always Flinders Street Station.

Melbourne's been a hotbed of teen-gang action since the Flinders Street clocks started ticking, larrikins, bodgies, rockers, sharps, b-boys, they all had their day as cock of the walk, and if there's one thing that connects them all it's those self same clocks. The steps up to Flinders street station, under the clocks, are the very heart of this blessed town, boss them and the city belongs to you.

The coffee bars of Swanston Street were much frequented by the sharps. You know the joints- booth seating, low potency coffee and if you find any food in your batter it's purely coincidental. The men in charge were generally hardboiled old Greek or Italian blokes, willing to put up with the occasional bout of rumbustials as long as the till kept ringing, but hell on wheels if you crossed the line. Swanston Street still boasts one or two old style coffee bars, virtually untouched by the passage of time. They've still got the mini jukeboxes at every table that used to blast out the latest Stones and Motown platters, and although there'd be new faces behind the counter I'd make book half of them are cut from the old cloth. I dare say the customers aren't quite as dapper as they were in '66 though.

Moomba and The Royal Melbourne Show were the biggest events on the sharpie calendar. Every year, from the sixties till the eighties, they exhibited and asserted themselves there en masse. Another occasion where the whole tribe mingled (and let loose an abundance of rowdyism) was the footy.

Denis
"Football was popular. We'd go to Richmond, Collingwood, North Melbourne, Windy Hill- all the grounds that are gone now. You'd go where the older fellas were going, hoping they'd notice you king-hit some goose."

Sharps always travelled by train, mostly because they were too young to drive. For many who grew up in the long-hair camp, weekend train rides into the city during this period are indelibly linked in memory to the threat (real or imagined) of copping a pasting from a gang of sharps, and it was always a gang, you'd rarely see a lone sharp.

On more than one occasion sharpie mobs set upon late night trams, relieved the driver of his duties, and rattled off on joy-rides, they actually stole trams!

Raising hell on public transport is all well and good for the young-uns, but there comes a time when a bloke needs wheels of his own. As soon as they were old enough most sharps bought cars, and Holdens were, of course, the machine of choice.

Peter
"I bought a car at eighteen, an FJ, everyone had FJ's. Mine cost seventy-five pounds, a luminous green shit-heap. Before any of us had our licences we'd all put in, raise forty pounds and buy a car from St George's Auto. Hillmans, Hudsons, we'd drive them till they fell apart. We bought a licence off some guy, they were just bits of paper back then. The licence said the owner wore glasses, so we kept a pair at hand and whenever the cops pulled us over whoever was driving had to stick them on. We had an old van in Footscray, it didn't run but we'd push it to dances, we used it as a mobile bed. We had a Hillman panel van and it was so bloody cold one night that we drove around with a fire going in the back, smoke bellowing out the windows...idiots."

Chris
"When I was about 16 I went to a dance called Traffik, a big sharpie hang-out, you took your life into your hands going there. There was a bunch of sharps out the front, older blokes, in

matching lowered H.D Holdens, maroon with white roofs."

A car and licence opened the door to a whole new life. Suddenly you weren't so shackled to the neighbourhood you lived in. You could go to any part of town you fancied without having to take on the locals. You were freed from the tyranny of the last bus home. Most significantly you could bend an elbow in any watering-hole you chose, legitimately. All this led to a lot of kids fading out of the scene.

Ken
"By the late sixties things were changing. We were older, had cars, girlfriends, our wages increased. We had more freedom, we were no longer just sharpies knocking around the streets."

In their late teens most sharpie blokes started feeling a yen to step out with a lady love on their arm, rather than with a pack of mug-lair cronies in tow. The calming influence of true romance put an end to many a sharpie bash-artist's reign. Back in the sixties most folks had tied the knot by the time they were twenty one, and the once-sharp were no exception.

Sinking piss with your mates and punching surfie teeth down surfie gullets is okay at 16 or 17, but after that your into your young-manhood, time to grow up and conquer those aggressive cravings.

Denis
"I hit a guy with a beer bottle outside a pub in Fairfield and I thought, I could've killed that guy and for what? That was the end for me, by this time the hippies had come along and they seemed to be having a lot more fun. A lot of my mates were just headed for jail, and I wasn't meeting any girls! You didn't have a hope with those morons around, probably didn't have a hope anyway."

The rise of Hippy played a significant role in the demise of the original sharpie scene. First off, there was flower power/psychedelia. In 1966/67 the pop world was taking off in all manner of new directions. Eastern music and philosophy, LSD, Tomorrow Never Knows. But flower power never really caught on in Australia, not to the degree it did overseas anyway. Things did change, in Melbourne dances were given new names more in keeping with the times: the Scene, a mod dance in Canterbury, became Lord John's, the Bowl became the Trip. Musicians started to experiment more, The Purple Hearts called it a day and Lobby re-emerged with the full-blown psychedelia of the Wild Cherries. Mod/stylist garb got wilder, more colourful, more effeminate. But for every kid game enough to don a kaftan and beads there were five sharpies to belt him for it. As Glen A Baker put it in his sleeve-notes for the excellent 'Down Under Dream Time' compilation: "Psychedelia was very much an alien concept in a frontier nation where brawling at a Saturday night suburban dance was closer to the prevailing community spirit than sniffing flowers or pondering Eastern philosophies."

Not our kind of clambake.

Psychedelia may not have been much of a goer down-under but it set the scene for Hippy, which, in the broadest sense of the word (long haired, hooch smoking, let-it all-hang-out rock fans) was very big indeed. By the end of the sixties, hippy had swamped the local scene, and a lot of sharp kids were growing their hair and bidding cheerio to the world of natty threads and blood n' guts street brawls. One feature of the hippy lifestyle in particular snagged a lot of sharp converts.

Arthur

"The fundamental change between '65 and '69 was, in a word, hashish. One of our boys brought some hash back from Sydney, he turned up at the pub with it and we had a few joints in his car. It made us all crook, we were all spewing up, and we just thought this stuff is hopeless, camel shit. The next night we rolled another joint, in a mate's bungalow, and this time it did the job, I laughed so much my jaw was aching. It used to be we'd be sitting around drinking, acting tough, and we'd decide to go belt someone- one of those Jordy Boys looked at me sideways last week, that sort of thing. We used to go to the Village Green Hotel in Glen Waverley and there'd be enormous fights, taking on other gangs, taking on the bouncers, unreal. But once you started smoking hash you'd get a little paranoid, thinking everyone was looking at you, start reading everybody's minds. You didn't really fancy fighting, you just wanted to lie around eating, giggling and listening to Hendrix. That's what wiped out sharpie."

By late '69 the sharp cult was running out of steam. For a few bitter-enders it was business as usual, but most had moved on. Some had married and settled down, some threw their lot in with the hippies, a goodly number were dodging bullets in Vietnam, and just between us kids, quite a few were in the clink. It looked like sharp was finished. But looks aren't everything. Fact is the end was a long way off, this was but a lull, a brief intermission. The torch was being passed to a new generation, the younger siblings of the original sharps. Before too long sharpie was back, in ultra deluxe form.

2

1970
-72

In 1969 there was much talk and tabloid ballyhoo about a new fashion being embraced by British teens. Skinhead, as the new cult was labelled, was an atavistic mod reaction to the 'summer of love'. Philosophically and sartorially skinheads, like sharpies, were straight as a Roman road. They spurned contemporary rock and it's high-art aspirations in favour of the more immediate pleasures of dance music, namely early reggae and U.S soul. Their look was mod stripped of all hints of decadence and ambiguity. Their immediate ancestors were the gang-mods, the kids who'd given the

rockers what-for a few years back. The gang-mods had been moving towards skinhead style since the mid-sixties but it wasn't until the turn of the decade, when the peace and love craze was sagging, that skinheads emerged as a force distinct from the mother cult. Indeed most of the earliest press write-ups on the new tribe referred to them as mods.

Skinhead style was crisp-cut and tough guy flash, very sharpie. During the day it was boots, braces, button-down shirts (checked or plain), cardigans and pull-overs, Fred Perry tennis shirts, jeans or Levis Sta-Prest, and Crombie overcoats. At night they went for tailored suits, brogue-patterned shoes, trilby hats and so on. Hair was, of course, cropped, but as often as not it was long enough to be parted.

Skinheads were generally working class, hooked on clothes, and loved to dance and fight. Sound familiar? Sharpies and skinheads were definitely cats of the same litter, they shared an origin in mod and a similar philosophy and aesthetic. The main difference was that sharpies gained a start on the skins by a good five years, chalk one up for the Aussies!

Although it'd been brewing for some years, the skinhead craze of '69 can be seen, at least in part, as a reaction to hippy-dom: its music, its fashion, its philosophy. Sharpies on the other hand were in business before the hippy thing kicked off, and did their level best to nip it in the bud back in '66.

Paul
"It started around 1969. You had 'Peanuts' who were the under Sixteens, and 'Hard-nuts' who were the older boys. I was from London, Harlesdon- a very rough area. There were a lot of West Indians turning up around that time, which was a big part of it. We'd hang around the West Indian record stores and try and pick up on their culture. It was very much 'black is cool'. I got around with about twenty guys, ten white guys and ten coloured guys like myself. It was about looking cool, a bit on par with the mod thing, very sharp, very clean cut.

Everyone was doing it. I don't remember it being a full-on battlefield, but it could get a bit ugly. Football was a huge catalyst. The weekend was dominated by football. We'd go to a school dance Saturday night, but we'd always get up Sunday for the game. Bands of skins would follow different London clubs and you had to watch which games you went to."

In July 1970, sixteen year old Chris Hall was bashed on a Sydney train by a gang of skinheads. The incident was widely covered in the papers and on the telly, and pretty soon everyone was talking about the new menace of skinhead-ism. Ian 'Molly' Meldrum, then tapping the keys for the pop weekly 'Go-Set', warned. "Skinheads in England attack anybody, they terrorise the general public, in trains, in theatres, in parks and at the football... Keep this type of violence out of Australia." Steady on digger!

As usual the media piled on the hype and hooey. There's no denying that British skinheads were rough company, but they weren't the mad-dog killers the gentlemen of the press and electronic media painted them as. If the media misrepresented the skinheads it didn't make the cult any less attractive to Australian kids, they read between the lines and sussed the fundamentals ie- skinhead means tough. British expat kids, from the hostels in Broadmeadows and Jordanville, were the first to sport the look in Melbourne. The style spread fast and pretty soon louts city-wide were running around with shorn top-ends and bovver boots. This slavish imitation of the British skinhead style was short lived but served as a catalyst for more interesting developments.

Chris
"I was a skinhead for a couple of months, this was '69/70. We all shaved our heads completely, got onto the white t-shirts, jeans and the bovver boots, all that caper. We bought the boots at the army disposals and they were so uncomfortable that after wear-

ing them around for a couple of days I thought- no wonder they want to kick heads in. Early 1970, when I was 17, I started hanging around Camberwell Junction, a lot of lads hung around there, mobs from Richmond, Malvern, Burwood, Hawthorn. A lot of my mates had older brothers who'd been sharps and after the skinhead thing we got into sharpie. By this time the original sharps had grown up and moved on. We didn't call ourselves sharpies but everyone else called us that, we wanted to be sharpies but to us the sharpie thing had finished. We'd heard stories about the big fights and all that. They were louts and that's what we wanted to be so we took a bit of their culture.

We got Cuban heeled shoes made at Venus, Kosmanos and Acropolis. The cardigan thing carried on, we didn't wear flags, although I had a pair, we mostly wore jeans, with a Crest-knit or a Penguin. The girls we hung out with wore pastel coloured 'Elta' cardigans, they were made by an old lady and had buttons shaped like bunnies. They also wore strap-on school shoes and later, clogs.

Most of the lout gangs in Melbourne had this look for the next few years until the second wave of sharps came along. By that stage most of my gang had grown their hair and started smoking hooch. We didn't like the new kids, they took the sharpie name but to me they weren't sharp, they were too extreme. On a good day there'd be eighty of us hanging around Camberwell, sixty lads, twenty girls. We'd drive around the suburbs looking for other sharpie gangs. Greensborough were a pretty big mob. Jordy sharps were notorious, they hung around the Matthew Flinders Hotel, we'd go down there and shoot at them with high powered air rifles, drive off in a hail of bottles and abuse."

The sharps of 1970/71 prepared the ground for the cult's second golden era. Sandwiched between sharpie's two major phases, they kissed off the out-dated aspects of the uniform, trilbies, trench-coats and whatnot, stripping back and re-modelling the style for the new decade. The look that emerged was leaner and more aggressive with a marked skinhead influence. The old short back and sides was ditched in favour of a short on top long at the back look- cut short on top, not cropped, and long at the back, as opposed to the thinned out rats tails that sprung up in '72. Although the final product was distinctly Australian, the Seventies sharpie haircut developed from a variety of overseas sources. British football hooligans went in for a similar, though less extreme, style after the skinhead look of '69/70 faded. British glam outfit Slade were sporting equally schizophrenic tresses around '71. Bowie got in on the act around '72. Another influence was the fashionable 'Dolly cut', a little longer and softer in effect.

The most significant addition made to the sharpie wardrobe in this period was the Conti Cardigan, or the Conny as it was quickly re-dubbed. Cardigans had been part of the sharp look since day one but Connys were elevated to a position of such super high eminence that they came to symbolise the cult. Made out Thornbury way, by a Greek gent named Mr Conti, Connys came in a variety of different styles. Some were round-necked, some v-necked, others had a crest-knit style collar. Some had thin pocket flaps on each side of the chest, most had five buttons and stripes of varying widths and colours. They always had a small belt buttoned at the base of the back, same size as the pocket flaps, about three inches long and one inch wide. In the beginning they were worn slim-fit (not spraycan-fit, that came later) and only by the lads. Originally sharps bought their Connys off the shelf, but pretty soon kids started bringing in their own designs, sparing no expense to wow their mates with new patterns and colour combinations. Soon a joint called 'Sam's Knitwear' in Coburg was bringing out similar designs and doing a likewise roaring trade. Cardigans made at Sam's were still called Connys, it didn't matter whether it was made by Conti, Sam or your Aunt Fanny, as long as it was exacto in regard to the essential details you called it a Conny.

1970/71 also saw the rise of the Q-Club (previously known as the Odd Mod) a dance, in the otherwise genteel suburb of Kew, that would become a popular hang-out for the next generation of sharps.

Chris
"Q-Club was the big sharpie place, it was where everything was settled because gangs from every suburb went there. We'd see Billy Thorpe, Ram Jam Big Band, Max Merrit, The New Dream, Cam-pact may have still been around. We didn't really go to see the band though, we went to hang out, look tough and start as much trouble as we could until the bouncers kicked our heads in. Bouncers in the seventies knew no mercy, they'd give you a kicking for dancing too enthusiastically."

The turn of the decade is always a time of tumult and change for popular culture, a time to scrutinise, define and label the trends, fashions and tenor of the past ten years. For some it's a time to toss aside those trends and fashions and get cracking at something new. But new trends take time to catch on and filter down from the pace-setters to the chain-stores, usually two or three years. Thus what we define as Seventies pop culture could be said to begin around 1972.....and how!

3

1972 -76

By '72/73 sharpie was once again *the* force in Melbourne's teenage world, with every young tough and would-be tough worth his salt donning the sharp garb and signing up with his local mob. But this was a new generation, mostly unaware of the cult's sixties beginnings. Mixing the stripped back style of '70/71 with a variety of contemporary influences, they came up with a look that was at once new and, at its core, true to the original aesthetic.

The short on top, long at back hairstyle of '70/71 evolved into the crop with thinned out tails. Tails were often bleached. Girls would usually have a short fringe and sometimes triggers- straggly bangs in front of the ears, often bleached as well.

Conny cardigans were now de rigueur for boys *and* girls, you'd wear them with a Crest-Knit/Banlon or a t-shirt and they had to be super-tight, just covering your forearms and midriff.

Julie
"The smaller you could get a cardigan and still get it on the better. We'd all go down the laundramat and wash and dry them till they shrunk."

Cliff
"I had about twenty Connys custom made over the years, cardigans, jumpers, short-sleeved tops. I always had them dry-cleaned, and folded them like they were in the shop- the right way. You could get any style you wanted. A mate of mine had one made with six belts running down the middle of his back. If someone tried on a cardigan from off the shelf Mr Conti would always click his fingers and say 'Justa right for you' no matter if it was too big or too small or whatever, that was his big saying."

Your Conny would just meet your high-waisted Staggers jeans at your belly button. Staggers were made by Joseph Saba, they were very flared and so snug around the hips and loins that many had to lie on their backs playing tug o' war with a coat hanger in their zipper to get them on.

Pinstripe and plain baggies (occasionally referred to as flags) were worn by both boys and girls. Baggies were high waisted and very flared, so flared that they'd cover the whole of your shoe.

Lee and Levis canvas were popular with the blokes, blue or black. Other brands like Amco and Wrangler were acceptable, but there were limits.

Mark
"The dead-set sharpie wore Lee or Levi's or Staggers, If you went to a concert in a pair of say, Boomerangs, forget it, you'd be asking for trouble."

Also sported were: wide, striped, button-on braces, worn over a t-shirt or a Ban-lon/Crest-Knit. Striped Conti V necks. Short sleeved gold thread Miller shirts. Flat caps. Lee Overalls. Singlets. Checked Lumber jackets with sheep skin lining, button-up was okay but for the real aces it had to be the zip-up motor-biking style. Dr Marten boots were worn by some, but the handmade brogue patterned shoes turned out by Venus and Acropolis remained the number one choice in footwear. Chisels gave way to more blunt shovel-toed numbers. Platforms caught on in a big way though some still opted for flat or Cuban heels. Kids still came up with their own variations on the basic design, red, blue, green and brown suede were common choices. A few flash characters got into the snake-skin and mock-croc. Needless to say there was still much tension but no fighting in the shoe shop.

Both boys and girls wore moccasins, the fluffy dyed sheepskin va-

riety. They weren't for occasions that demanded your best bib and tucker, but if your evenings activities consisted of hanging around the local shops sinking piss, moccasins were A.O.K. Smart kids had leather soles stuck on them for added durability.

Treads- sandals with brightly coloured suede uppers and soles cut from car tyres, were an equally popular and unlikely choice in sharp footwear, unlikely because they were very much part of the surfie uniform at the time, and the seventies sharps, like their sixties forebears, hated surfies something murderous.

Everybody got into iron-on letters, the kind a small time footy team might stick on t-shirts to get a uniform happening. Sharps would get their gang's name stuck on one side and maybe their nicknames on the other. Alternately they'd get 'Bowie' or 'Lobby' or what have you. Girls wore them so itsy-bitsy and tight around the balcony that the letters would inevitably split and fall off. Matching t-shirts made you look and feel like an army- touch one touch all. Each gang had their own variation on colour and design, for example, Melbourne Sharps- white t-shirts with black lettering on the back, West-side Sharps- blue t-shirts with white lettering on the front. If you fronted a dance mob-strong you'd wear your gang t-shirts with pride. If you found yourself surrounded by superior forces you'd turn them inside out quick smart.

Tattoos were still a sharp essential.

Bob
"There were only three tattooists that I knew of. John Entwhistle, Dickie Reynolds who was next to the Waterside Inn, up a rickety old staircase, always up there drinking a cup of tea but I'm sure it had scotch in it, lovely old bloke, could talk under water with a mouth full of marbles. Then there was Tex, a relative newcomer, up the other end of Lonsdale Street, notorious for tattooing fourteen-year-old boys like me. Dickie Reynolds only asked me how old I was once, on my eighteenth birthday, and he'd already tattooed me four times."

Stars were a favourite. Australians have been adorning their anatomies with star tattoos since the wild colonial days. In the London criminal underworld, from whence many of our forbears were plucked, placement and number of stars denoted which gang you kept company with. Most sharps had a star tattoo somewhere on their person- fingers, wrist, earlobes, usually just a wee bit smaller than an old one cent piece.

Bluebirds, skull and crossbones, knives, and the love/hate knuckle biz were also big. A few heavy-duty blokes got neck tattoos, some of the A.N.A's, a crew from out West, got their gang name done, but the classic choice was 'cut here'. D.I.Y jobs were common, 'sharps' or 'skins' or your nickname.

You'd do them with a needle and Indian Ink, and if you got bored with them you'd remove them by rubbing a match head on them till the skin was red-raw, then rubbing salt into them. Some kids cut their gang's name into their arm with a razor blade. A lot of blokes who'd been in Turana carved Charlie Manson crosses into their heads. Some of the older sharps had prison tats- beauty spots and what have you.

If you really wanted to dress to kill, a suit was still the way to go. Suit jackets were invariably pin-stripe and worn with matching baggies and an open necked body shirt. They were generally double breasted, slim-fit and flared at the hips, with a single vent and a Conny style belt at the back, very zoot suit, very Bowie circa 'Pin-Ups'. By the early seventies, sharpies in suits were a rare sight indeed. But then, the amount of blokes wearing suits period had dropped enormously since the days, ten years earlier, when a man who didn't own a suit and hat would've been judged some kind of dangerous bohemian nut. You were probably more likely to see sharpie girls in suits than you were the blokes, either way it was always in the above style, sometimes tailor made, sometimes bought from the Myers 'In-Gear' shop.

The new breed of sharpettes wore a lot of the same gear as the fellas- Connys, Crest-knits, Treads, Staggers. Their hair varied from short with fringe, tails, and sometimes triggers, to a Bowie cut. It was acceptable for girls to keep their hair long, but look sharp in every other respect. Boys

generally had to play it all or nothing, but girls could dabble, particularly if they were blessed with the kind of qualities and developments that young men admire.

Make-up was plastered on, particularly around the eyes, every colour of eye-shadow and mascara was employed. Eyebrows were plucked pencil thin, some girls used Nair and lost them for keeps. Lipstick was pale. Nail polish was black, silver or iridescent greens and blues, sometimes in stripes.

The fashionable sharp sheilas wardrobe included: baggies- brown with gold pinstripe, or satin- sometimes with matching jacket (cropped, zip-up). Skirts- mini's (usually denim) or long pencil numbers, satin or pinstripe. Halter neck tops. A-line/V neck pinafore tent dresses, three-quarter length with three-quarter sleeves, usually corduroy, worn with a polyester body-shirt, or a tight thin-ribbed polo-neck. Other A-line dresses - navy with white cuffs and collar and big white buttons etc. Tight striped t-shirts. Brightly coloured stockings. Bobby socks (with minis) and rainbow stripe socks. Cork-soled platform shoes.

Julie

"The cork shoes had six-inch soles all the way along. When you bought a pair you had to go out and scrub them on the road to try and get some grip, otherwise you'd slip and kill yourself."

Accessories: a choker with your initials on it, lots of bangles, a handbag (wedged firmly under your arm).

Shops like 'Merrivale' and 'In-Gear' were much frequented by those who's tastes ran to the lurex and satin end of things.

Glam Rock, particularly David Bowie and Slade, had a tremendous influence on sharp. Bowie had been at it since the mid-sixties scoring a monster hit with "Space Oddity" in '69, but it wasn't till '72 and the release of his 'The Rise And Fall Of Ziggy Stardust And The Spiders From Mars' LP that he really seized centre stage. In '72 rock music was on a 'progressive' anti-pop trip, high-toned and drug-numbed. That was okay if you dug that kind of thing, but not everyone did. Many wanted something with a bit of sass, a bit of violence. Bowie fit the bill and then some.

Aussie kids went mad for Ziggy, none more so than the sharps. Bowie's proclamations of sexual versatility meant diddly-shit to most sharps. They just wanted a big beat and a lively show, a Bowie speciality.

Concept albums, that is albums made up of thematically linked songs, were all the go in the late sixties and early seventies. Some of them were good, but just as many were god-awful, full of over-blown quasi-classical tripe. 'Ziggy Stardust' was definitely a concept album, but contained within its grooves was catchy, crunchy beat music of the kind that had been mostly stuck in mothballs since '67, rock n' roll for spruced-up Saturday nights, exactly what sharpies had always gone in for.

Marc Bolan was another sharp favourite.

Inspired by Bowie, a lot of sharpies, especially the girls, dyed their hair green, blue and most commonly Ziggy red. Some would even dye stripes through their hair.

The eyebrow plucking and rainbow make-up of sharpie girls was probably partly inspired by the Ziggy look as well. A few sharpie *lads* got into the make-up too.

Sammy
"Some sharps wore make-up. I remember seeing some at the football wearing eye-liner, mascara, blush, rouge, it was the glam influence."

Lisa
"There were lots of sharpie boys who dressed like little Bowies, Ziggy Stardust look, androgynous, glam."

In the early seventies it was possible to be a tough guy and look, as the times would've had it, like a poof. Mind you, you had to be bloody tough!

Rather than a crop and tails a lot of sharpies went for a Bowie cut, short at the sides, spiked up on top and long at the back. For the total look you'd dye it red as well. Often kids with this cut were branded 'Bowies'. Being a Bowie was a good compromise if you wanted to be a sharpie but your parents wouldn't let you get the haircut. One ex-sharp told me of a time his mother crept into his bedroom while he was catching some winks and cut off his tails with a pair of scissors, what a terror! There was also the Droog look. Droogs wore sharpie gear and knocked around with sharpies but had a similar haircut to Bowies, not necessarily dyed or spiky, just a kind of grown out crop and tails.

Most sharps sported Droog or Bowie cuts at one time or another, particularly if they had to front court.

The Droog moniker comes from the Anthony Burgess novel 'A Clockwork Orange', Stanley Kubrick's 1971 film version being every sharpie's favourite movie. The Droogs of 'A Clockwork Orange' are a vicious teenage gang, decked out in bowler hats and white boiler suits. 'A Clockwork Orange' was very popular with British skinheads and quite a few of them took to dressing like the film's protagonists. In Melbourne we had the Oak Park Boot Boys, a Clockwork Orange inspired wrecking crew from the Western suburbs- more about them later.

Media hoopla about supposed copy-cat crimes caused Kubrick to withdraw the film from distribution in early '74, but for some reason it continued to screen in Australia, becoming a midnight movie mainstay for the next twenty-five years.

In the wake of Bowie and Bolan's success every dog and his brother wanted to hitch a ride on the Glam gravy train. All the Glam groups won a corner of the sharpie market: Gary Glitter, Wizzard, Alex Harvey, the regal Mott the Hoople, the Chinn/Chapman stable of Mud, Sweet and Suzi Quatro, the urbane Roxy, Cockney Rebel and Sparks; yanks like Alice Cooper, Lou Reed, Iggy Pop, Kiss and Brownsville Station.

But the band that really made off with their hearts was Slade. Like Bowie, Slade had been hawking their wares since the mid-sixties, releasing records as The N'Betweens and Ambrose Slade to little buyer turnout.

Things started happening for them in 1969 when they took on former Animals bass player Chas Chandler as their manager. Chandler persuaded the group to adopt a boots and braces image to win over the skinhead audience and grab some publicity. They got publicity, but their sound at the time was closer to the Yardbirds with a dollop of Lennon and McCartney than anything skinheads wanted to hear, and promoters, equating skinheads with trouble, wouldn't touch the band.

An obvious parallel can be drawn between Slade's attempts to curry favour with the skins, and the fledgling Who's efforts to cast themselves as four hep young mods. The Who were never genuine mods, but they were definitely in tune with the mod idea. Likewise Slade were never true-blue skinheads, but with their council estate kidhoods and booze n' birds image, it was clear they marched to the same drum.

By '71 when Slade scored their first top twenty hit with a raucous cover of the Little Richard oldie 'Get Down And Get With It' their stage-togs had changed considerably. Front man Noddy Holder, decked out in an oversized flat cap, bright yellow braces, tartan strides that fell way short of meeting his ankles and a whopping pair of red platform clodhoppers was the very model of the new look, part skinhead, part glam colour riot. Slade were glam, but they were nobody's idea of androgynous. To them glam was just fashionable razzamataz. At heart they were meat and potatoes rock n' roll. And they were massive. Between '72 and '75 they were the most successful chart act in Britain, winning over teeny-bopper and terrace-rowdy alike.

By '72 skinhead was pretty much kaput in Britain, replaced first by the suedehead, then the smooth/boot-boy. Suedeheads were a more dapper, less aggressive looking lot than the skins. Their hair was generally long enough to be parted, their rig-out was hard-mod swank- no boots and braces for these gents, strictly custom built suiting, loafers, button down shirts, the kind of gear skinheads had saved for painting the town.

The suedehead look then gave way to the smooth/boot-boy look-

longer hair in a shaggy Rod Stewart style, tank-tops, baggies. Superficially it was all a far cry from the lean mean look of '69, but really it was the same old story: flash threads, football, scrapping and music.

Back in '69 English skinheads had eschewed rock music in favour of reggae and soul, finding the late sixties progressive groups a pompous yawn, but glam was different, danceable, to the point. A lot of boot-boys dug it. It never came close to usurping black music's place in their hearts, but for many (mostly youngsters) it became their bit on the side.

At the time of their January '73 Australian tour, Slade held the top three places on the national singles charts and the top two on the album charts. Their Sydney and Melbourne shows pulled in close to thirty thousand punters each, even though it rained like a bastard on both days. Propping up the bill were Lindisfarne, Caravan and Status Quo, but in all fairness they were just side dishes, Slade were the real meal. No sane person would've endured a three hour down pour for Lindisfarne, believe you me. The concerts attracted every sharp and skinhead in the country

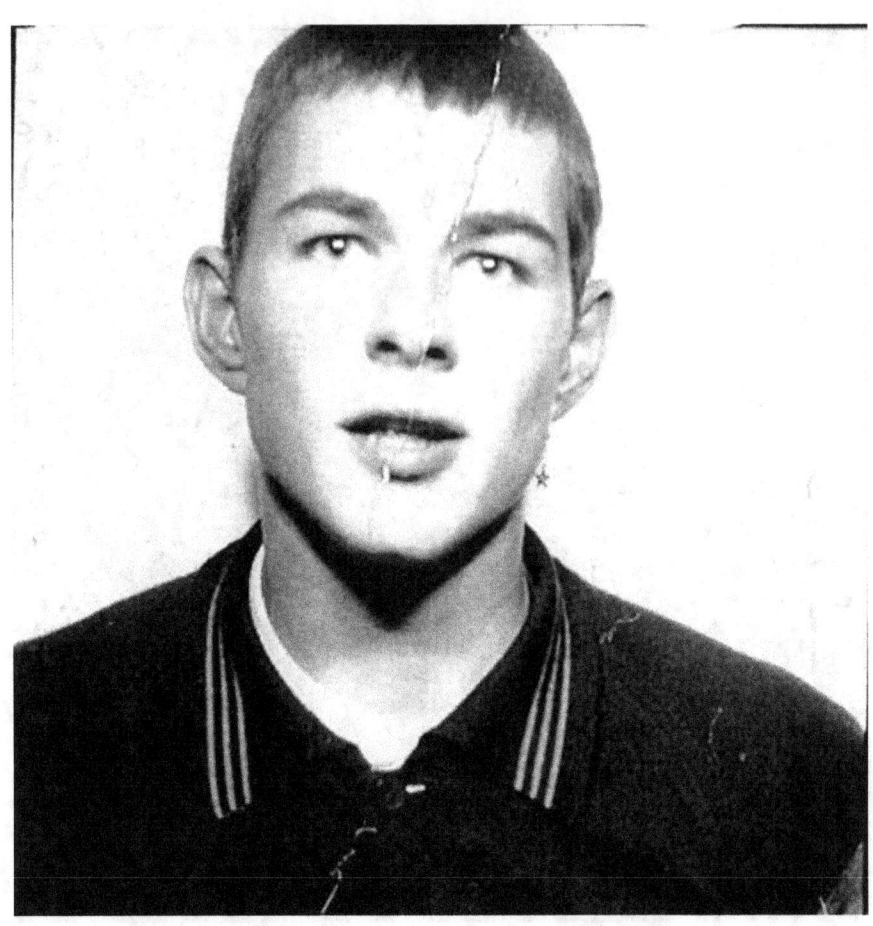

and there's some great footage, shot for a T.V show called G.T.K, of a sharpie stage invasion at the Sydney Randwick Racecourse show.

As you would expect there was a fair bit of aggro at the Slade concerts, but it was nothing compared to what went down at a free concert held on Boxing Day '72 at the Frankston Football ground.

Frankston was always a sharp stronghold. In the Sixties Frankston sharps regularly battled it out with the Chelt Boys, whose leader was the legendary King Fist- Tony to his mum. In the mid-seventies all the mobs in the area banded together as the Bayside Sharps, probably the biggest gang in the South East.

Twenty security guards from the Bob Jones karate school were hired to keep the concert booze free and bounce any troublemakers. There were rivers of bad blood between the sharps and the Bob Jones blokes. The Jones boys bounced most concerts and dances and were notorious for their enthusiasm for knocking heads, especially sharpie heads.

Cliff
"The Bob Jones school was in Elizabeth Street, so you'd get

these guys who'd do six or eight lessons then come down to Flinders Street and start with the skinheads. It got pretty full on."

Chris
"I was at an AC/DC concert, when they were first starting out. There would have been about sixty people in the audience and thirty of the Bob Jones boys, and they just attacked, literally punched up the whole crowd."

The concert kicked off at 9 A.M. Groups booked to play included Blackfeather, Murtceps and Sherbert. Over twenty thousand kids turned up, including a number of sharps, how many exactly I really couldn't say. I've heard there were at least two hundred and I've also heard there were less than twenty, so who knows. By midday, thanks to a number of successful smuggling operations, half the crowd were pissed and things got wild. The story goes that the sharps got stuck into the Jones boys, the crowd got fired up, and it was on, the biggest knock down drag-out in the history of Oz rock concert violence, and it's a pretty blood-soaked history! At the height of the fighting one thousand people are supposed to have been bopping into each other. The Jones boys got clobbered and fifty kids were arrested. The incident made all the papers and Bob Jones, the man himself, had this to say: "The trouble seeking kids wear their hair short on top and long at the back and they are heavily tattooed. They are a revival of the sharpie element of five years ago and have been stirring trouble around the discotheques in the past two months... My chaps never hit anybody, I teach them not to get rough but to create good relations with the young crowds." Concert crowds were pretty rough back then and you needed real hard men to keep the peace. Unfortunately how to keep the peace was a bit of grey area. By all accounts some of Bob's boys were a tad bash happy.

Ironic sidenote number one: a few years down the track Bob's daughter Tracy joined the sharpie ranks. Ironic sidenote number two: a hell of a lot of sharpies ended up bouncers.

The 1972 Sunbury pop festival was also the site of much hellacious brawling. Some of it involved sharps but mostly it was longhair V longhair. Billy Thorpe was without a doubt the man of the moment, and it was his devoted disciples, the 'suck-more-piss' brigade, that were responsible for most of the fighting. These blokes liked drinking beer. The only thing they liked more than drinking beer was drinking lots of beer. They were no more peace and love than the sharps, and indeed quite a lot of them were ex-sharps.

Billy Thorpe is a bona-fide institution, one of the best-loved rock n' roll singers this country has ever produced. From the beat-pop sixties through the blues-thunder seventies Thorpie and his Aztec cohorts commanded a massive, fanatical following, a large number of whom were of the sharp persuasion. In the early seventies the Aztecs were the country's foremost concert attraction. They made some pretty good records, but their brand of unruly, up-and-at-em R&B was best experienced live and L-O-U-D. Aztecs at the Opera House, Aztecs at Sunbury, Aztecs at the Myer Music Bowl, these were landmark moments in Australian rock n' roll. Billy Thorpe has a relationship with a generation of Australians, a place in their hearts, that few can rival.

The 'Skinhead' books by Richard Allen were another big influence on the seventies sharps. Richard Allen was really Canadian born James Moffet, a prolific writer of pulp fiction. Moffet was commissioned by publishers New English Library to come up with a penny dreadful to cash in on the British skinhead craze. The resulting product 'Skinhead' hit the shelves in 1970 and sold truckloads, inspiring Moffet/Allen to write sixteen follow-ups. The series includes such gems as 'Top Gear Skin', concerning, shit you not, skinhead stock car drivers, and, milking two cash cows with one pearl of a book, 'Dragon Skins', a kung fu/skinhead concoction that's impossibly absurd.

The central character of 'Skinhead', and several of the subsequent books, is a chap called Joe Hawkins, a scurvy knave if ever there was one. Joe bashes and roots his way through various adventures, finally meeting his maker in the totally abysmal 'Skinhead Farewell' (1974). Joe being such a high-speed troubleman you'd reckon he'd get killed in a gangland shoot out, a bungled robbery or, with his habit of diddling in the hay with other fellas' fillies, maybe at the hands of a jealous beau or hubbie. But no, Joe is killed in a plane crash returning home from a sojourn in, of all places, Perth Western Australia!

The 'Skinhead' books are Spillane style thick-ear pulp, all willing women and crunching bones. They're full of right wing bullshit and sexist unpleasantries, get steadfastly worse as the series progresses and have sweet Fatty Arbuckle to do with your genuine article skinheads. But they have great covers! And it was the cover snaps, real live British skinheads decked out in the latest threads, that were the books' biggest selling point with the sharps.

To the average Aussie, skinheads and sharpies were like ground hogs and prairie dogs- different handle, same critter. Was there a difference? Yes and no, it's a knotty question. The press played a major role in confusing the matter. Some people never tire of hearing about what a rotten pack of wastrels the 'the youth of today' are. Thus the press will always try and sell the latest youth cult as the last word in moral degeneration. The old sour-pusses lap it up, and most young people don't buy newspapers so who gives a funny valentine about them. Skinheads were the big hubbub in Blighty and the Aussie press obviously wanted to cash in. Sharpies were yesterday's news so most reports on sharp gang clashes in the seventies ran under headlines that screamed skinhead. When 'A Clockwork Orange' was big news the papers labelled all sharp activities as the work of droogs.

The straight-up British skinhead style was briefly popular in Melbourne at the start of the seven-

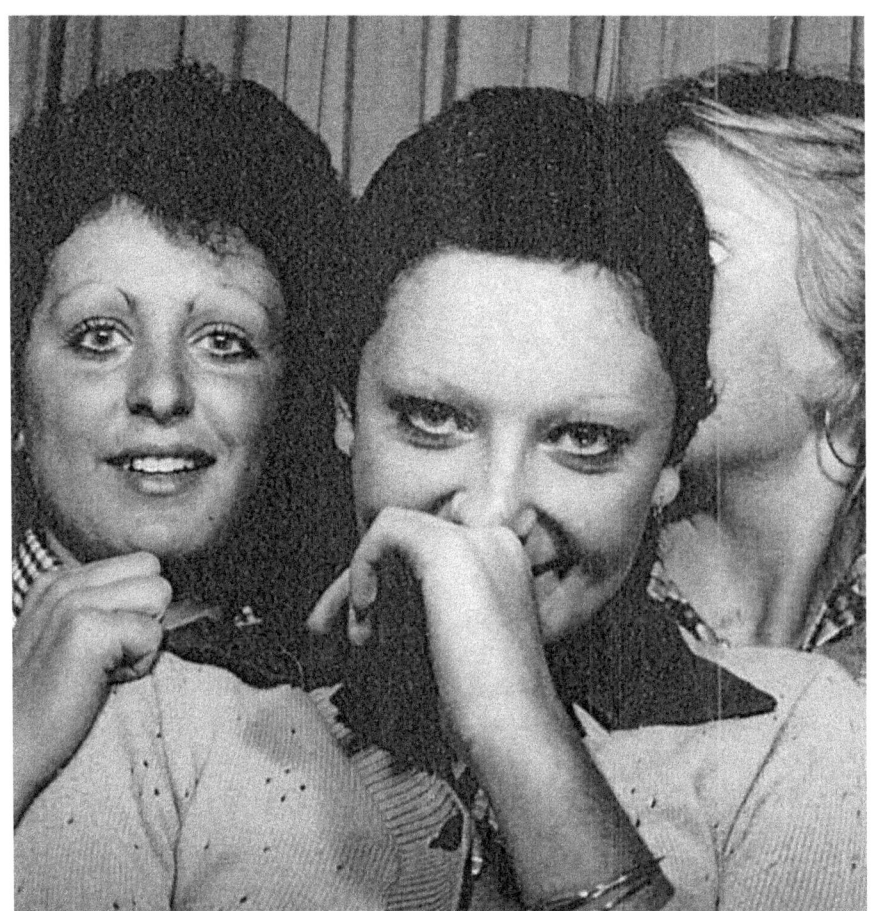

ties. It was soon swallowed up by the growing sharpie revival and the two styles blended into one. But the skinhead name endured, particularly in the media, and there was much confusion, even within the sharpie ranks, over what the difference between skinheads and sharpies was, if indeed there was a difference. There were several takes on the issue. For most kids it was half a dozen of one six of the other- they didn't really give a hoop-de-do. Others will tell you that sharps had tails while skins didn't, fair enough, but then you'd be just as likely to find blokes with tails who called themselves skins and others without tails who called themselves sharps. Another theory was that skinheads were heavier than sharps, less into the glam fashion, more into punching on, but there were too many skinhead Bowie nuts, and too many five-star bruisers that classed themselves as sharpies for that theory to hold water. Fact is, some kids called themselves sharps, and others skins, it all boiled down to where you were from and who you knocked around with, and the difference added up to nothing much at all.

That this new generation should adopt the sharpie name was a source of great annoyance to many of the original sharps. From where they stood, only a jump from teen-hood themselves, yet often married with kids and the whole grown-up shebang, it probably looked like their youth was being stolen from them. But whatever they called themselves they *were* sharpies, British skinhead was but an influence.

The chief element separating Australian sharpies/skinheads from their British brethren was music. The Brits went in for reggae and soul, the Aussies, rock n' roll.

The British skinhead cult was the rendezvous where working-class English and Afro-Caribbean culture conglomerated. In comparison, these shores saw little Afro-Caribbean migration and thus, save for Tamla Motown, which always teetered on the brink of being pop music anyway (no slur), contemporary black music never really caught on with seventies Australia, sharpies included. You would've needed a long day's rummage to unearth it, but the sharps of the seventies still had a fair sized streak of rocker in their make-up.

Melbourne's not New York, there's only so many places where you can hobnob, come to blows or get a pair of shoes made. Consequently, sharps of the sixties, seventies and eighties lurked a lot of the same turf.

The city coffee bars remained a popular sharp meeting place into the early seventies. Known in sharp parlance as wog shops, spag bars or chat n' spews (the latter because most had names like 'Sit n' Chat' or 'Chat n' Chew') these joints were sharp central, so much so that the press dubbed the area 'Skinhead Strip'. The most popular coffee bar was the Quick, situated on Flinders Street, next to Young and Jacksons.

But by midway up the seventies sharpies were, thanks to their mischief making, persona non grata at The Quick. Most of the other coffee bars followed suit, going as far as putting 'no sharps or skinheads' signs in their windows, and (according to The Truth) serving sour milk coffees to sharps who attempted to defy the ban! The blackguards!

A few doors down from The Quick on Flinders Street was Mutual Bowls, a bowling alley cum pinball joint where sharps could always be found. Shindig, a weekend dance at the Mordiallic Life Saving Club, was another hot spot.

Bob
"Shindig was like neutral territory, you'd go there Sunday night and it would be rockers, sharps, surfies and there'd never be any trouble- you'd play table tennis with them."

Other popular haunts included pinny/pool joints like Alfies in Market Lane (now Ding Dong Lounge), The Leisure Centre in Elizabeth Street, Ringwood Ice-rink (where you could catch live bands like AC/DC) and the Saint Moritz Ice-rink in St Kilda- sharp infested from the cult's earliest days. Umpteen hours were spent in skate-rinks and bowling alleys, but nobody bowled or skated, they just

hung out, played the pinnies, looked tough and smoked.

Saturday arvo most crews would make an appearance at Flinders Street Station, just like back in the sixties. You'd scan the pack for anyone you owed a biffing, powwow with mates from other neighbourhoods, and find out what was on the cards for that night in the way of dances, parties or fights. From '72 to '75 one mob bossed Flinders Street from arsehole to breakfast time. They were the very legendary Melbourne Sharps.

Bob
"Melbourne Sharps was a conglomeration of kids from different areas, Box Hill, Altona, Dandenong, Heidelberg, Moorabin, Preston, everywhere. I got into sharpie late '72, early days. I met these blokes from Heidelberg at a concert, they had the Connys, grey with red stripes, short hair with tails at the back, they looked fantastic I said 'how do I join'. I met up with them in Preston, got me cardigan, got me hair cut- did it myself, shocking job, had huge chunks sticking out

of my head. I went to a barber in Barkly Street, he said 'Mate, that's not a haircut it's a repair job' and charged me fifty cents. One Friday night we were dagging around, nothing to do, so we caught a train from Bentleigh to the City. We're standing on the steps at Flinders street and a couple of babes walked past, didn't call them babes then, probably called them molls, they had the short hair with rat-tails, platform shoes, Connys, short pleated dresses. We told them to round up all their mates and meet us there next Friday. We ran into about ten more sharps and told them the same. The next Friday there was thirty or forty of us, the week after a hundred, the week after two hundred, the week after three hundred. The cops didn't know what to do, we weren't doing anything, just hanging around, but they had the riot squad there, thirty cop cars. When Melbourne Sharps was at its peak it was everybody, a thousand people, there were other gangs, but they'd mostly put their differences aside."

Julie

"One P.M Saturday, down to Flinders Street, it took one person to start something and it was on, all in punch on, you shook hands at the end of the day though. I don't know why we all decided to belt each other up, it was just one of those things, you were trying to prove yourself, stand up for what you were- what that was I have no idea. You had certain places where you stood at Flinders Street, mine was third step down on the left, near the hat shop."

Tony

"The City thing started from Q-Club. If you were a skinhead and you went to the city on a Friday or Saturday night you were going for one reason- and it wasn't for the pictures- another group would come along, and try you. We were magnets for trouble. You had to be very careful where you went. We ran a lot, sometimes we'd turn around and fight too, but five guys against three carloads, there's nothing you can do. So the city thing was like all the smaller gangs that hung around Q-Club getting together, groups from all over. Fifty, sixty kids is a little more imposing than five. Nobody's going to pick you."

Boxing remained big with sharps, but not to the degree it had been in the sixties. Its popularity was challenged somewhat by kung fu, all the rage thanks to the Bruce Lee films. The sharp lads worshipped Bruce for obvious reasons i.e.- he could really go in the arse-kicking department. Most sharps figured kung fu as a handy tool to blue with. A few got right into it and could deal out kung fu castigation with the best of them. But the majority were totally lacking in the discipline training in the martial arts demands, they just picked up moves here and there and mostly, they posed. Sharps had plenty of fun with the hardware of kung fu as well, nunchukas and all that gear. Needless to say you don't need to put in ten years training to spoil somebody's day with a pair of nunchukas. The influence of kung fu on the girl-sharps was mostly stylistic. Chinese silk happy coats came into vogue, as did jade rings and Chinese lettering on chokers and earrings.

Most sharps, boys and girls, wore earrings, either studs- plain or sometimes star shaped, or sleepers- plain gold or with tiny hanging bells, crosses, bluebirds, and even brightly coloured Ronnie Wood style feathers. Many had multiple piercings, but for the boys only on the left ear, earrings on the right ear meant you were gay, having both ears pierced meant you rated yourself a top fighter and would take on all-comers. You'd always take your earrings out before a blue. Everyone knew that the best way to fell a sharp was go for his earrings or tails. If you had him on the ropes and really wanted to shit on his head you'd rip the belt off his Conny.

In '73/74 sharp was the number one teen fashion in Victoria, long-hairs don't count because everyone had long hair, it meant nothing. Sharp squads ran things North, South, East and West, even country kids gave it a burl!

Chris
"We saw AC/DC play in Poowong, back when they were just starting. There were a bunch of sharpies there, Poowong Sharps, had the t-shirts with the iron on letters: this is in a town with one pub and one shop. They're walking around like they own the place and I'm thinking, jeez, how'd they ever get onto it here."

It's fair to say that, like their sixties counterparts, seventies sharps were more than somewhat prone to punching on. They fought each other, neighbourhood against neighbourhood, they fought rockers and they fought surfies.

Mark
"We didn't like rockers, we had no reason really, but they were rockers and we were sharpies and we knew that rockers and sharpies didn't like each other."

There were plenty of good natured kids in the sharp ranks that disliked fighting. But whether you liked fighting or not it was hard to avoid. Often times you'd get carloads of blokes, rockers or surfies or just plain louts, who'd set upon sharpies simply because they wanted a fight and were bloody well gonna get one. In that kind of situation it's fight or be fought, and you'll come off a lot less bruised if you take the first option. You might say that they could've avoided the situation altogether by dropping the sharpie image but you'd be missing the point.

For a lot of these kids sharpie was their whole life, if they had to scrap for it they would.

Bob
"They were strange days. There was a bunch of guys called the Bentleigh Bashers, they'd been around since the sixties, some of them were rockers, some were just louts. They used to drive around the suburbs looking for people to beat the crap out of. Their leader was a guy named Empty Head. He later joined the merchant navy. Last time I saw him he was driving down Centre Road in East Bentleigh in an MC Holden with no doors or windscreen, screaming his head off."

Surfies were usually down the coast 'shooting the breakers' or whatever it is they do, and fighting was never really the be all and end all for them, though when the occasion arose they applied themselves to the task with great vim, believe you me. Rockers on the other hand hung around the same suburban skate rinks, bowling alleys and coffee bars as the sharps did and sharp/rocker clashes were common. Fifties nostalgia was rife in the early seventies. The essence of it was most likely exhaustion. After all the calamity of the sixties, rock n' roll's protoplasmic age probably looked like a pretty nice place to visit, particularly if you donned the proverbial rose coloured glasses. Rocker activity had never fully died in Melbourne but the revival of interest in fifties rock and fashion was definitely a shot in the arm for the cult and their numbers

rose substantially. They were never a real threat to the sharps, but they kept them on their toes.

Adelaide was where rocker really happened. Adelaide's rockers were partly cast from the classic mould and partly something new and, for my money, sharpie influenced. The look, head to toe, was this: hair quiffed or simply slicked back. Multiple earrings. Threads were black: skin-tight Lee or Levis, mesh t-shirts or singlets, sometimes set off with a red neck scarf or a crucifix. Most important was a pair of black suede ripple soled desert boots. Ripples were to the Adelaide rockers what Connys were to Melbourne's sharps, a symbol of your allegiance to the cult. So synonymous were ripples with rockers that a mate of mine was knocked back from an Adelaide nightspot because he was sporting a pair, and this was in the early nineties, ages after rocker had bitten the dust. Musically the Adelaide rockers went in for Kush, AC/DC, the same kind of stuff the sharps rated, indeed there were quite a few ex-sharps in the rocker ranks, many of whom originally hailed from Melbourne. This didn't mean that everything was cosy-cool between Adelaide's rocker and sharpie populations, far from it, the two camps were sworn enemies and squared off regularly.

On the whole sharps ruled the roost in Melbourne, but in some neighbourhoods the rockers more than gave them a run for their money.

Sam

"I went to Jordy Tech in '73/74, at that time I'd say a third of the school were sharpies. Jordy Skins was made up of people from Jordanville, Holmesglen, Waverley, Box Hill and Ashwood but it all happened in Holmesglen, the Matthew Flinders pub, always thirty or forty kids hanging around. I lived in Chadstone and that was mostly ethnic/rockers, Greeks and Italians, slick hair, pointy shoes, all dressed in black. Once you crossed Waverley road you were into the Housing Commission district and that was Anglo/sharpie, there were ethnic sharpies though, and the ones that I knew were real ballbreakers, believe me. There was a lot of conflict between the rockers and sharps, more than there was sharp against sharp. If a sharp went to Oakleigh, or a rocker went to Jordanville there'd be trouble. I was left alone because I knew a lot of rockers. All the sharps would have to go the Oakleigh pool because there was no pool on their side, so the pool would be totally split, one side rockers, the other sharps. The Oakleigh Rockers were the big rocker gang, later on they became the Oakleigh Wogs."

Which brings us to the gangs whose identities were derived, in the main, from their shared ethnic backgrounds. These gangs first appeared in the mid-seventies, chief among them were the Black Dragons and the Lebanese Tigers. The Black Dragons were a mob of Turkish blokes who were into body-building and Tai Kwon Do. Most of them came from the Western suburbs, Dallas, Broady, a few from Richmond and Collingwood. They dressed, naturally, in black: baggy kung fu daks, satin bomber jackets, t-shirts emblazoned with their dragon symbol. They dug disco, hung out at clubs like Snoopys and Crystal T's and were said to deal pot and pills. The Lebanese Tigers were a similar proposition. They wore black t-shirts with tiger head designs on them. Legend says they used to sit in the City Square psyching out the competition with Arab chanting routines, which is possibly -probably- bullshit, but it's a cute anecdote. Neither outfit was known for their lamb-like gentility and sharps were their pet aversion. The hate ran high.

There was no racism involved in the hostilities, most sharp mobs were mixed grills ethnically, and there were definitely sharps from Turkish and Lebanese backgrounds. The aim was to be the number one crew, clear the decks of all contenders. Be you Turkish, Greek, Shanty Irish or Pig Latin, nobody gave a rusty fug, it was purely territorial, tribal.

The last twenty years has seen the rise of a new kind of skinhead, ultra right-wing, racist, bearing little resemblance to the original skins in style or philosophy. These guys are always in the papers so to your average citizen skinhead equals racist. Often seventies skins and sharps are retrospectively tarred with the same brush- an infamous slur! Sharpie first manifested itself in areas like Coburg, Brunswick and Collingwood, areas with large migrant communities. From the start sharp gangs were half and half jumbles of Anglo and Mediterranean kids. Back in the sixties there were more than a few Koori sharps knocking around as well, so the idea that sharp was an Anglo only affair just doesn't wash. Fact is, in their day sharps were the most ethnically diverse crowd around, no competition.

Mick
"Sharpies were a real ethnic mix, Anglo/Celtic, Greeks, Italians, Turks, Yugoslavs, joining sharp gangs was an Australianisation process for a lot of kids."

Everybody had a nick name- take a bow Ugly, Scoota, Radar, Glider, Wormy, Weasel, Buster, Mouse, Little

Mouse, Ace and Penguin. Often kids got around in twosomes and were nick-named accordingly- Horror and Terror, Pixie and Dixie.

Then there was Chopper. You know his name, you know his fame.

In 1991 Mark 'Chopper' Read set about recording his experiences as Australia's most infamous stand-over man. The resulting book 'From the Inside' was a fascinating and often funny account of a life lived outside the law and behind the high grey walls of the prison system. 'From the Inside' established Chopper as a national celebrity cum big bad wolf. The books have come thick and fast since then, just short of a dozen last time I looked. If you ask me he's a far better writer than many would credit, and a humourist of no small talent. 'Gluttony and the Gourmet Crim' in his fourth book is a brilliant piece of work.

Alphonse Gangitano 'The de Niro of Lygon Street' was also a sharp in the early seventies. Allegedly involved in a number of illegal gambling and standover operations Gangitano was shot dead in his Doncaster home in 1998.

Not every sharpie lout graduated to full-blown crim-hood, the majority got jobs, got married, had kids, became all-round upright citizens. A few even fell in with the boys in blue!

Garry

"I got into sharpie when I was fourteen, around '73. I was from Dandenong West, the group of blokes I used to knock around with were from Lindale, Doveton, and all about. We used to meet at the 'Pot Black' pool-room in Dandenong. Sometimes the local rocker gang would come down, and we'd have a bit of a tango, but there really weren't many groups in the area that would touch us. We were the big boys, if you know what I'm saying. We had a terrible reputation and there were plenty of fist-fights and bashings, but it was considered absolutely filthy to use your boots. If you fought you fought clean and if you lost you lost, you didn't pull out a knife or a machete. It's a pity the gangs of today don't operate under a similar code.

I got out of it when I was eighteen. It seemed at the time that it was going to be jail or a life in the pubs, so along with two of my mates, I joined, would you believe, the police force, which led to some very embarrassing situations. I was stationed at Dandenong and a number of times old mates of mine were brought in to station. One bloke told the sergeant he knew me and would only speak to me, told him I'd been the best man at his wedding, of course he's got a sheet of priors as long as your arm. I felt as big as thruppence."

Dancing remained a big part of sharpie life. The first couple of rows of any halfway decent rock gig were inevitably taken up by a slew of dancing sharps, all bobbing heads, hunched swinging shoulders, pumping elbows and suggestive hand gestures. I could expend a dozen lexicons and still not clue you to the genius of seventies sharpie dancing. All I can suggest is that you ply your ex-sharp aunt/uncle with intoxicating beverages, slap on a Thorpie long-player and demand a demonstration.

The local bands that made a hit with the seventies sharps fit loosely into three categories: the no-b.s boogie rockers- Thorpie, Buster Brown, Blackfeather, Sid Rumpo and Texas, the glam-*pop* top-tenners- Skyhooks and Hush, and the second-flight glam-*rock* bands- Redhouse Roll Band and Cloud 9/Taste. Fat Daddy and AC/DC sat somewhere in between, gun-barrel-straight rockers yet, if not quite glam, more than a wee bit theatrical. The mould-breaking Kush stood way out in left field- jazz-rock fronted by a Ziggy-oid singer with a Teddy Pendergrass voice.

Max Vella (Fat Daddy)

"I was from Footscray and there was a lot of heavy guys around. Most of the Footscray crims were sharps and they took a real pride in the way they dressed. It was a real gangster mentality, you had to look the part. Being a musician you could avoid the fighting and still be respected, because the sharpies and skinheads congregated around the bands. Music soothed the savage beasts. I didn't like the violence, but the fashion sucked me in. Also, if you wanted to have anything to do with Western Suburbs girls you had be a skinhead.

You had the Williamstown Boys, the Sunshine Boys, the Braybrook Boys, all on the same train line. You had to watch what carriage you got on when you were coming home from the city. There were no automatic doors then, and kids got thrown off trains.

I got bashed badly by the Williamstown Boys. Afterwards I went up to American Billiards, where the Footscray Skins hung out. Within half an hour there was one hundred guys headed for Williamstown for the payback. That's how crazy it was.

Most of those guys got locked up. Some of them got into heroin and are dead. That was the way Footscray was back then. You went to work at the market, or the abattoir, and then you hung out on the main strip and got into fights. There was nothing else to do. There were only two TV stations! Australia was just a big country town. It was a scary time for teenagers. But then, you'd run into some of the heaviest guys a few years later, guys who'd carried guns, and they were the nicest guys around, big pot-heads.

Fat Daddy had a big sharpie following, we were all from the Western Suburbs and they were our mates. Fat Daddy were originally called Fat Mama, they were a three piece group with Tony Catz on guitar and a female drummer called Lynne. They split up in '74. Before they split Tony agreed to play some gigs in Sale, which was a big skinhead town. At the time I had a band called 'Iron Stag', with Mick Stilo on bass. We were all 14/15, a real skinhead band. We rehearsed in Mick's family's garage in Avondale Heights. Mick was Italian and his father would slaughter pigs in the garage, so there were intestines all over the walls. We were strictly a garage band, never played a gig. A few girls would come and watch us, and we'd drink Mick's dad's homemade wine. We were forced into letting some of the real heavy skins be lead-singers. None of them could sing but we had to use them. Tony came to see us, wanting to put together a band to play the gigs in Sale. That was the start of Fat Daddy.

We used to wear these grotesque masks. We were anti the whole pretty boy/satin/ Sherbert thing. We wanted to be the ugliest band in the world. We got it from the wrestling- The Masked Musicians. We used to play our

own support slots, unmasked. We called ourselves 'The Flying Fungool Brothers', we played country rock, Lynyrd Skynyrd kind of stuff. We'd get booed off. Then we'd go backstage, put on the masks, come out and play our usual stuff and they loved us.

The sharpies were real crazy, if they didn't like you they'd spit and throw things at you. One time we played a dance in Chelsea and a girl spat at Mick, who then threw a glass of orange juice on her, all over her satin jacket. After the dance there was at least one hundred and fifty skins waiting to beat the fuck out of us. We got changed, took the masks off and looked pretty much the same as they did- walked straight past them. We'd play places like The Cage at the Christian Brothers' College in Yarraville, and there'd be a thousand sharps and skins. At Ormond Hall in Prahran you'd get surfies and sharps, and there were some very ugly fights. But it wasn't all violence, there was also a lot of fashion, parading around with that gay sort of walk they used to have. Fat Daddy evolved into Texas because we wanted to get rid of the masks, we wanted the girls to know who we were! Texas were a hard hitting ZZ Top style boogie band, people used to call us ZZ Wog. The skins loved us, the Hells Angels loved us and the industry loved us. AC/DC, Cold Chisel and Skyhooks were all fans. We were the under-dogs who never quite made it, a bunch of wog-boys from the Western Suburbs. We had the meanest skinhead roadie crew you could imagine- Big George, Froggo, Mad George, Beaky, Saucy- all notorious Western Suburbs skinheads. Nobody fucked with us."

Roosting at the top of the sharpie-rock heap were Lobby Loyde and the Coloured Balls. They owned the times. Lobby Loyde is largest rock n' roll talent this country has ever produced. By a great many lengths. For first-ear evidence hunt up a copy of 'Ball Power', the Coloured Ball's debut platter. Nice little record. Rocks like the hammers of hell.

Lobby wasn't the only marvel in the Coloured Balls arsenal, the rest of the band deserve a lifetime supply of pats on the back as well. But Lobby was the headman, the mouthpiece, for the band and for the whole sharp tribe.

In their day the Balls stood alone, before the Birdmen, before the Seedies, they were Australia's sole purveyors of high-energy, gut level, punk rock n' roll. There wasn't a combo in the kingdom with a spoonful of what they had, not a hint, not a particle. The Balls' only real peers in sound and vision were overseas- the Detroit axis of The Stooges, MC5, et al, and the amphetamine space-rock of British groups like Hawkwind, The Pink Fairies and The Deviants. The main difference between The Balls and these groups is that The Balls have never really been given their due, which as a fan, and as an Aussie, cheeses me off no end. Even in Australia they've been denied the kind of retrospective accolades hurled at AC/DC and Radio Birdman; yet they were a better band, more uniquely Australian than the Birdmen and more unique full-stop than both groups.

LOBBY LOYDE

"I'm from Central Queensland, the country. When I was young I went to the city for education and to play rock n' roll- I heard Elvis and Gene Vincent and Buddy Holly and that was it. My peer group all wanted to play music and we were pretty much focused on that. I've known Bill Thorpe since he was a kid. When we were kids in Brisbane our mob was me, him and Barry Gibb. We all played rock n' roll and we were in competition with one another. The two little nerd Gibb brothers, we used to hate those little turds and we'd try and get Barry to leave them at home. Every time those pricks entered a talent quest they'd win. Thorpe was always the loudest singer I've ever heard in my life. He was two foot tall when he was young and he always had the ability walk on stage and command the audience to obey him.

My first band were the Devil's Disciples, I played piano. This was Brisbane in the Fifties, they were a bunch of biker type guys who had an old fashioned rock n' roll band and they needed a piano player. When I was young I could play all that Jerry Lee Lewis/Fats Domino type stuff, couldn't play it now for the life of me, that's RSI territory, like playing drums with your fingers, and it hurts. Playing every Saturday night with them I met other guys. I met a guy called Errol Romain, weird guy. You couldn't buy solid body guitars in those days, you had to make them yourself, and this guy was really good at it. He needed a bass player so he made me a bass, copied from a picture of an American band. I played bass with him for a while, but secretly I wanted to play guitar because that was the instrument I could hear in my head. I went into a music store and I was standing there with a pink 'Strat' in my hands, this guy approached me and asked me if I played guitar, being an idiot I said yes. He was looking for a guitarist, doing auditions in three weeks. He gave me a list of all the songs they played so I went and bought the records, sat down with a guitar and learnt to play them by ear. I turned up to the audition thinking I didn't stand a chance, but I turned out to be the best guitarist there, and I taught myself to play in three weeks! The band was 'Bobby Sharp and the Stillettos' great name, has an Italian sort of ring to it. Their lead singer had the full Elvis haircut, big side-burns, the whole caper. Everyone in the band had copious quantities of quiff, I didn't really fit in because I'd been playing with a bunch of bikers, I was kind of hairy, my hair was going one way theirs was going the other.

Then I joined the Purple Hearts, who were then called The Impacts. Their guitarist fell in love with a girl from Melbourne and went off on her trail. They needed a guitarist to fill in while he was away, just a short-term job, three or four weeks. A year later I'm still in the band and we got the Rolling Stones tour. There were three pommies and me. Because they were straight from the English scene they had records by bands I'd never heard of, English R&B. All you heard in Brisbane was the top 40, which was whatever was selling in America. We got the Stones gig in Brisbane but the promoter said that if we wanted to play Melbourne we'd have to change our name because there was a Melbourne band called the Impacts. One of the guys from the Stones said, referring to Purple Hearts, 'You guys eat enough of those you should call yourselves that'. You'd buy Purple Hearts from the chemist shop, six shillings for a bottle of fifty, people virtually saw them as confectionary, or like 'No-Doze'. So we became the Purple Hearts as a joke, we used to say we were named after a medal of valour. For some reason as soon as we changed the name the attitude in the band changed as well, we took on a harder edge, still bluesy but harder. When we came to Melbourne we realised we were kind of unique. Most Melbourne bands were top 40 covers bands. Melbourne was split into jazzers, surfies, mods and the early sharpies. It was quite strange because everywhere you went there were jazz bands. Trad jazz was massive in Melbourne. We'd play gigs as the rock band playing with two jazz bands. Most of the guys from the Seekers came from the Trad jazz scene, so did the Loved-Ones, they were the Red Onions Jazz band. The Loved-Ones were quite similar to the Purple Hearts, similar vocal style similar attitude. We became the best of

buds because we were both fish out of water in the scene at the time, but we both hit a nerve with the audience.

When the Purple Hearts first came down to Melbourne we were a long haired blues band. We started playing the Circle Ballroom in Preston and places like that, and I started noticing all these strange people. I'd never seen anything like them, a distinct style. They had short hair and wore baggy trousers and cardigans, the girls wore Knee-length pleated skirts, twin-sets and pearls. They really liked the music, were incredible to play to, and had their own way of dancing, they were just fabulous. I saw a few alarming incidents at the Circle. In those days you had Rockers and Jazzers and both those crews hated Sharpies. They'd turn up in great big herds and wait for the dance to end so they could belt the hell out of everyone coming out.

As the Sixties went on the Purple Hearts broke up and I started playing with the Wild Cherries at The Thumpin' Tum, The Biting Eye and all those places. The guys in the Purple Hearts got all the latest records sent to them from their relatives in England. We got all the Who stuff, the Graham Bond Organisation, all the underground stuff. One guy we knew was working as an engineer at Track studios and he sent us one of the five test pressings of the first Jimi Hendrix album. It was a white label and we didn't know what it was. I whacked it on in a room full of musos, 'Foxy Lady' started and all heads turned, jaws dropped, we nearly died.

We picked up on the freedom of the playing in the new English and American sounds. That's why the Wild Cherries were probably a little further on edge than the Purple Hearts. You wouldn't know that from the Wild Cherries records because we still had to make records in conservative Australian studios, with pretty square engineers, but live we were quite an experience. One of the most exciting bands I ever played with. We had a keyboard player named Les Gilbert who couldn't buy half the stuff he wanted so he built it. He chopped a cello down, turned it into a bass guitar with piano strings, built his own Leslie cabinets; one of those guys who was winning piano eisteddfods when he was six, bit of a nutty genius. We had an English drummer called Keith Barber and a great singer, Dan Robinson, who also played upright bass and harpsichord and studied classical music. A guy from Queensland called John Phillips was on bass. We used to go on stage with a rough framework and just go for it, kind of free-form.

Being in the Aztecs was the other side of the road because when Bill came down here he'd been through the big fame trip and he'd come out wanting to play in blues rock band. It was quite a relief after the chaos of the Wild Cherries to play rock n' roll and R&B again, it was like going back to The Purple Hearts. They needed me because they couldn't arrange for shit, and if you're going to play blues and rock n' roll you've got to turn it around a bit and make it your own, otherwise it's back to covers again. It was a good time, but I ended up wanting to play more hard-edged full on music. The MC5 and people like that were doing it, and I wanted to do it too. The MC5 and the Stooges I liked because they were grunty. The MC5 were interesting, not just their music but the interviews, the articles, they were like an explosion. Even their manager went to jail! Old Sinclair, he was a bad-man. I was listening to the MC5 while I was in the Aztecs, and I'm thinking- hey man, what's happening, I'm in Australia playing pub-rock, and these guys are going ' let's take the world!' They definitely influenced me, politically and philosophically more than musically, because I was already kind of edgy like that inside myself. As a muso, there was this real loud raucous bastard living inside me. I sort of stopped noticing sharpies when I was in the Aztecs because the Aztecs were a pub rock-band. That was our first priority, a super loud, super drunk band. In the meantime a whole new generation had come through and the fashions had evolved. I formed the Coloured Balls because I liked what I was seeing. I was fascinated by it, I thought it was a very romantic movement. I liked the way they looked, the way they danced, the whole vibe. The Coloured Balls were a bit more frenetic, jumpy, we'd drifted more into that style of things, rhythmic. The Coloured Balls became one of the few bands who could communicate with these kids. Everywhere we played would be full of them, they liked our music and we liked playing to them. The media picked up on it and started calling it a violent movement. Sure there's always troublemakers in every scene, and peripheral aggression, but that's youth, that's exuberance. My memory of the era is of a kind of super-Australianess, that's what it was to me. The main reason I broke the band up was that a few journalists started saying that the Coloured Balls were a band that encouraged violence, which is rubbish, listen to 'God' or 'Human Being'. The pleasure kind of went out of it then, and I think it was the same for a lot of the people involved because nobody wants to be branded with a reputation they don't deserve. To me all the girls looked like Minnie Mouse, with their big cork shoes and their short skirts. They didn't look like a bunch of villains out to create havoc- they looked like a bunch of people off to a fashion show. I remember it as a good period. I'm probably not the best person to speak about it because I was a fan of it, I saw it as something far more romantic than maybe a lot of other people did. A lot of people may dispute what I say, some of the dedicated hard-edge sharps, but I'm speaking about what I generally saw, essentially a fashion movement. I'm sure there were elements in there that were aggressive, because there are in every teenage movement. When I was young it was impossible for outsiders to walk around Redfern or Paddington in Sydney, they were no-go zones because of the razor gangs. They only became trendy boutique areas in the 1980's, if it wasn't for the hippy movement I don't think it would have changed.

Other musicians despised the Coloured Balls, I was always getting advice from friends like 'Why don't you play some real music?' and ' You're a good

BALL POWER
COLOURED BALLS

muso, what are you playing this garbage for?' I'd say 'because I like it'.

I think that throughout history, the dances of the people have always fuelled the rhythms of the musicians. It's pretty hard to ignore an audience, if you're looking at an audience and they've got a certain rhythmic thing, you'll find yourself playing it or not playing there anymore. I liked the way the sharpies danced, the rhythm and the visual, so I wrote music that went with it. If you go back through American music, swing, be-bop, I guarantee you it all goes back to the audience. Okay, a guy sits in a little back room and comes up with a new revolutionary form of jazz. He goes to a little club and maybe he finds an audience, but that's the one out of ten. I reckon the nine out of ten is people responding to their environment.

A lot of musos round the scene didn't want to let go of the hippy movement, because they'd found their glory in it. They had the Jackson Browne approach to music- they tried to put the lounge room on stage. They saw the Coloured Balls as pretty poxy.

Most live bands are a totally different deal to recorded bands, live you're here and now, you're not planning. I've always preferred the live scene. Recording music this year and putting it out next year with a big advertising campaign is not what immediate music is all about. It's about responding to your audience.

I can honestly say that the Coloured Balls didn't give a stuff about the industry. All we cared about was the people who came to the gigs, and the industry gave us heaps over it, they said we were thick, that we could turn what we had into something. We used to say this is something, it's good, it's what we do, and we don't want to turn it into anything else. The record company in Sydney did their level best to stop us making anymore of 'those crappy records' as they put it.

When we sent them 'Ball Power' they said 'that's crap' but what stunned them was it went into the top five in Melbourne in the second week of release. It even went into the national charts, which meant it was selling in cities that didn't even have a sharpie thing. EMI, when we sent them 'Ball Power', sent us a 10CC record and said that was what they wanted us to sound like. That's why we jokingly made 'Love You Babe', that was kind of our laugh at them, and they said 'Oh thank you, that's much better'. 'Ball Power' and 'Heavy Metal Kid' are it, we made them exactly like we wanted to and then got the hell out of there because they weren't going to let us make any more. The writing was on the wall. They were saying 'We'll have to get you a real producer for your next record'. A 'real producer' is someone who works for the record company whose job is to 'Take this bunch of lemons and turn them into a nice product that we can sell'.

I've always thought the producer should be there to protect the band from the record company, but the modern idea of a producer is a guy that protects the record company from the band.

I ended up producing Buster Brown because they were in a similar vein to us. They were playing to the same sort of people we were, and I liked them. When I first met Angry he was Gary. He became Angry because it was the thing, everyone was Warty, Cranky, Farty or something. Angry has always been a street guy. He was always intense, always related directly to that vibe. Angry is a unique guy, he's ballsy, he'll go out and say what he thinks and do what he can. He just looks kind of

weird, two feet tall, covered in tatoos, bald, but I find that attractive about the guy. Phil Rudd went from Buster Brown to the Coloured Balls and then to AC/DC, he was with us in our final phase and he was an energy ball to play with.

I went to London at the end of the Coloured Balls, I made 'Obsecration' and went to London, trying to get away and have a bit of a rest. I went with plans to stay two weeks and stayed until '79. I was in the U.K when Joe Strummer was in The 101ers, and Glen Matlock was in the The Pistols. I thought this is it, this is where the Australian scene was trying to go but the industry wouldn't let it. The industry tried to hold it back, make it conservative, as they always do. I've always figured Australia's problem is this: a great act comes along and the record company says 'We like your crowds guys, what we don't like is your music and the way you look, so if we could just change all that and get a nice producer in to re-write your songs...'

What I loved about England is that when the new wave happened they embraced it, they said this is interesting, this is exciting. I remember, in the Coloured Balls days, industry people told me that after the Beatles and the Stones and all the American bands, groups were finished, there was nothing left to do- acoustic singer/songwriter stuff was the future. I would have loved to get them down the 100 Club a few years later, they would have killed themselves, all their dreams shattered. Some of the Coloured Balls best songs were two minutes long and I was pretty impressed when I heard Wire, and all those groups that came after the Pistols. They made albums and the longest song would be two minutes, and I thought 'Hey, that's what I wanted to do'. The Coloured Balls had a lot of build-up songs that we'd do live, stuff like 'God'. The sharps would do dance routines to them and to watch it you'd think you were at the New York Metropolitan watching some bizarre modern ballet. That was great, but the other side of me wanted to make two or three minute blitzkriegs that went a million miles per hour, but we were thwarted by record companies.

When I was in London one of my friends sent me a copy of 'Bad Boy For Love' and told me it was an Australian punk band.

Somehow Rose Tattoo had been branded punk when really they were just streets hard rock n' roll. The only band I ever saw in Australia that could truly be called a punk band were X, they were it, there was nothing else. They were bloody alarming, a fundamentally exciting band. All the other bands like Radio Birdman and all those guys, mate, I don't care what anyone says, that's a kind of Aussie music that you don't hear anywhere else, it's one of the unique things about this country. AC/DC and a few other bands changed the way every heavy metal band in the world plays, they added that edge of aggression that us Aussies are pretty good at.

When I came back from England I recorded an album with Gavin Carrol and Gil Matthews, the drummer with the Aztecs, called 'Live with Dubs'. Angry came down and did some vocals for 'Gypsy in my soul', purely for pleasure. Most things I do in music are purely for pleasure. Some musicians plot a distinct path from the opening, others just play for the moment. I definitely fit into the latter category. I don't think I've ever planned anything and I'm not likely to start, I'm a bit old for that.

The terrible thing about becoming old is that you're still inquisitive, but your so far out of things that you no longer have the luxury of sliding into scenes to look at things and see what's going down. I'm an old nerd now, I walk into interesting places and they wonder why I'm there. They think you must be a drug dealer a weirdo or a pervert."

In 1973 Sharpies second golden age was in full swing. Lobby was the Godhead, Q-Club was the place to be, and a good two-fisted time was had by all.

Daryl Braithwaite (Ex-Sherbert)
"It was intense, scary. If you were playing certain gigs you didn't know if you'd come out alive. Q-Club was one of those places, there was always fights there, always, but never anything directed at the bands, just between the gangs."

Tony
"The big thing was Lobby Loyde at Q-Club. The place would be full, eight hundred people, all skinheads. Madder Lake were quite well liked, as was Thorpie, but Lobby was idolised. Why would we want to go see Spectrum? Why would we want to go see Daddy Cool? Those guys had long hair, but Lobby, he looked like us. If you could go and see Lobby every weekend you would. It was like Lobby was to us what Koutoufedes was to Carlton supporters. Q-Club was like a big family, if you were a regular you were looked after. But outside groups would come to fight. There were fights every week. A lot of times it was older guys. They'd turn up afterwards, two or three carloads of them, five or six in each car, and they'd chase you. They were the proper boys, in their twenties, very scary. They were there to hurt people, whereas a lot of the regulars were there for the music and the

fun. One night outside Q-Club forty or so Richmond and Collingwood boys turned up and took everybody on. They were karate guys, they hit the bouncers first and then just came through like a wave, put down everybody. I've never seen so much blood in my life. It wasn't just fists, they were armed, pickets stuff like that, and they didn't stop, if someone went down that's when the boots came out. It was like watching two football teams going at it hammer and tongs."

After Q-Club closed down the action moved to 'Canopus', a weekly dance held at Box Hill town hall.

Chris
"When Q-Club finished Box Hill became the big thing. They'd wreck the train on the way up, then it would be on for young and old. They seemed intent on maximum destruction."

Edwina
"Someone always got punched up at Canopus. You'd be doing your skinhead dance with your handbags in the centre, and

these boys would come in and dance on someone, pummel them on the dance floor. It was almost part of the dance."

Ken Murdock (Ex-Cloud 9/Taste/Texas)
"We played with AC/DC and Lobby Loyde a lot- places like Saint Peters dance in Bentleigh, Ormond Hall in Prahran, Box Hill town hall. That's where you'd get the sharpies. We had a sharpie following but I could never understand why because a lot of the time we'd get into fights with those guys. They were always pushing, very violent. I can remember kicking a few of them with my platforms, hitting them with mic stands, I always thought the stage was my domain and if they crossed that line...but they didn't lynch us so maybe they did like us."

Bob
"I got a job bouncing on the door at Box Hill, got my teeth knocked out by some guy I wouldn't let in, I opened the door to let someone else in an he punched me in the mouth. There was always one or two ratbags and some trouble, but nothing you wouldn't get with any large group of kids."

Anytime the Coloured Balls played Canopus, or Sirius as it was later renamed, they'd pull in between one and two thousand kids, mostly sharps. The local cops weren't too keen on having half the city's juvenile delinquents landing on their burg every weekend, and did their best to wet blanket proceedings, stopping trains bound for Box Hill and ousting any Conny clad kids.

The gutter press launched an attack on the dance. Sharps had always been good copy. Slow news days in the early seventies often meant headlines warning of imminent sharpie/biker wars and other such bullshit, and it was bullshit, no sane sharp would've dreamt of tangling with anything resembling a bikie.

In '73 the Sunday Press ran a front page story claiming a brawl at Canopus had escalated into a 'skinhead rampage' through the streets of Box Hill. More bullshit. According to the article the riot had ended with more than twenty kids arrested, but when pop paper Go-Set followed up the story they found that the police knew nothing about the supposed riot. Fact is the kids were pretty quiet that night. They weren't sitting around playing patty cake patty cake, but there wasn't much rampaging going on either. Canopus promoter John Abbot did his best to counter the negative publicity, taking his side of the story to the more credible papers, but the damage was done. The weekend after the first report, TV tabloid perrenials 'A Current Affair' darkened the Canopus portals, hoping the sharps would lay on some pandemonium for the cameras. They went home empty handed. All eyes were fastened on the dance- the cops, the media, local residents - and the sharps stayed away in droves.

On the night of the riot-that-never-was the Coloured Balls and the Aztecs topped the Canopus bill.

the Aztecs were a big draw with the sharps but the Balls were supreme, so when the tabloid shit-storm hit, it was Lobby who copped it.

The Coloured Balls were branded public enemy number one.

In '74 The Coloured Balls released their second album 'Heavy Metal Kid', but it was obvious that the end was nigh. By the end of the year the band had split. Industry hostility, bad press, gig violence, they'd had a gutful. The greatest rock n' roll band to ever stalk this sunburnt country, shot down at the height of their powers.

After the Coloured Balls chucked it in two new bands took over as the top sharp live-draws, AC/DC and Skyhooks.

AC/DC got together in '74 and right from the first they were men with a mission: to drag rock n' roll back to it's snarling disreputable roots. They mixed Fifties rock, the blues, the sneeringest-leeringest edges of sixties British R&B, and the Marshall stack thunder of post Zep rock and came up with a sound as

simple as it was brilliant, the giddy limit of balls-out no-brow rock n' roll.

In Bon Scott they had a frontman of immeasurable star quality, with a voice so whiskified and slithering he could've recited a row of words from 'The Magic Faraway Tree' and still have sounded like a black-hearted jackal. The Sharp world was immediately smitten with the Seedies, and Bon Scott was a big part of the appeal.

Julie
"Bon Scott was the epitome of what we stood for, he was rough, he was tough, and he didn't care, that sneer! A nasty Elvis, a rebel, a god, he stood for trouble. You heard about the Stones, but they were the other side of the world, we couldn't comprehend Perth, AC/DC were ours."

In the seventies the nation's top pop units toured the suburbs, playing 'Zodiac' dances, babels of pashing and bashing organised by adults who wanted to chaperone their children's debauchery. 'Zodiac' dances took place in high school lunch breaks (not so much pashing and bashing) or on the weekend in a local hall (heaps of pashing and bashing). AC/DC quickly became the top dogs of this circuit. When AC/DC played even the most dedicated waggers fronted school. The weekend dances meant getting pissed beforehand and punching-on afterwards. As often as not the sharps couldn't wait and would start roughing things up during the concert, a situation that didn't faze bands like AC/DC too much.

Sam
"I saw AC/DC in Oakleigh in '74. That night the Holmesglen skins got into a biff and it was on, with Bon Scott and the lot of them. Bon came out with the microphone stand, they weren't scared of having a bit of a rumble."

Cliff
"I was in Holmesglen Skins. There was a core of about ten of us who'd hang around the Matthew Flinders Hotel. AC/DC played there one night and we tried to pull Angus off the stage. We thought he was a cocky little shit. He mentions it in one of the books, says he got his fingers broken. That was our claim to fame, that and, I think, second page of the Herald- Youths Harass Man On Train."

AC/DC were so revered by sharps (Holmesglen Skins excepted) that even the most trifling connection with the band was enough to give you instant A-list standing.

Virginia
"AC/DC were the icons, a friend of mine went out with an AC/DC roadie, that was a big honour."

Sammy
"Knowing a cousin of someone from AC/DC was prestige, up there with knowing someone who'd been in Turana."

The filming of the promo clip for the Seedies 'Long way to the top' single was the big moment. You know it: Bon and the boys motoring down Swanston Street on the back of a truck. Everybody was there, or so they say. It's one

of those epoch defining happenings that everyone claims to have been at. But if everyone who says they were there, was there, the street would've been swamped thick as downtown Delhi and the truck wouldn't have been able to move an inch. Gang, I'm sceptical.

And then there were the Hooks. In their chart topping heyday Skyhooks had an enormous sharpie following. Skyhooks always put on a show, something scant few bands were interested in back in the days of heads down 'progressive' rock. It was appreciated. They had great songs too, concentrated bundles of melody and wit, another scarce commodity at the time. They sang about Toorak posers and Lygon Street after dark, they sang about what they saw. These were Melbourne boys, from the suburbs, and they made no bones about it, they celebrated it.

Mark
"Skyhooks weren't a hard rock band, but we still liked them. It was their lyrics, songs about Carlton, dealing, down to earth sort of stuff, we loved it."

In '74 came 'Living In The Seventies' the Hooks debut platter, every cut championship material (well almost every cut, 'Motorcycle Bitch' is a tad hows-your-father). Half the album was banned from the airwaves but it didn't matter, it sold like crazy, lapping the field like no local group since the days of 'Easy Fever'. One thing the Hooks had over the other Category-A sharpie groups was that they appealed to girls, that is they were photogenic enough to win over the 'Spunky' readers, your teeny-bopper bracket. Of course there were thousands of young ladies who would've given their eye-teeth for a ciggy-tongued pash session with Phil Rudd, but it's fair to say that Phil, Angry, Bobsie and the rest had a more specialised appeal. More for your wayward numbers, your hell's belles. Your common or garden suburban popette was much more likely to get all swoony over Shirley Strachan who was, for all his front, a nice Mount Waverley surfer boy and cherubic as all heck. Skyhooks were the point where sharpie met teeny-bopper, the catalyst for a lot of teenage girls getting into sharp. These were not the hardboiled sharp molls of lore and legend, the chicks with bricks in their handbags, coat-hangers up their sleeves and 'fuck you' scowls, these were not those girls. These were girls who lived for 'Countdown' and dreamt of candle-lit dinners with Les Gock. Pop sharpies! Not that they were all that innocent, they weren't Sherbert fans! They wagged school and dared each other into shop lifting, but at the end of the day they were just 'normal' teenage girls looking for a little danger and excitement.

GREG MACAINSH

"I thought sharpie was visually very interesting, very stylish, and I don't think there's been a youth cult since that's been that unified.

The first time I ran into sharpies was in the mid-sixties. I used to go into the city to see bands. I was brought up in Warrandyte so there was a bit of a tyranny of distance there. I remember waiting in the queue outside a dance called the Catcher, I was, I guess, a mod, at least I had long-ish hair, and the sharpies were out to get anyone like that. I was playing in a band at the time and a couple of the guys in it were sharpies. They lived in Preston, they wore the flared Italian trousers and the knitted tops. This was a high school band, The Sound Pump, I think. There were a few other bands who had that look, Les Stacpool and the Browns, some others. Later on I used to go and see Billy Thorpe and Madder Lake, the long-hair bands. Skyhooks were a bit of a reaction to that, I got a bit bored with it after I saw Gary Glitter, that really changed my perspective on music and show-biz and what it could be. '73 I was a hippy, long shoulder length hair. Then I started Skyhooks and, influenced by the sharpie thing, I cut it short leaving it long at the back. Steve Hill, the original singer, was very much into sharpie, he was a bit of a sharp, had the hair, liked the aggressive thing.

When we first started we played a little bit with the Coloured balls, the first gig Shirley Strachan did with us was supporting Lobby at the Frankston Police Boy's Club. We used to go and play in the Western suburbs, which I think was one of the good things about us. Even though we were inner-city, in the sense that we played Unis and Red and Steve lived in Carlton, we'd take all these gigs out in the burbs. I remember going to play some place in St Albans and thinking we'd definitely get punched up because we were kind of glam and there was no security or anything, just a little church hall. After the gig these guys came up, shook our hands and said 'not bad mate'. They were all in Lobby Loyde t-shirts and a year later they were all Skyhooks fans.

We played with Buster Brown a few times, at the Chelsea Civic Centre, and on a Mushroom package tour. Angry had the rats tails, the Pentridge cut I called it. We played Pentridge a couple of times, Steve Hill organised it, I think he had some friends inside. We played in B Division, long term heavy stuff, and of course there were tons of sharpies in there. They'd all just sit and watch, two hundred guys, nobody danced or anything.

There was a big sharpie presence at our concerts, particularly girls. I remember we played a football field in Sunshine and got mobbed by sharpie girls, there were tons of them, we couldn't get out.

The back cover of 'Living In The Seventies' is absolutely supposed to be sharpies, because that was the crowd in the suburbs. The guy who did it was a mate of Red's from Carlton. The place is modelled on a place we used to play at called Ormand Hall on Mobray Street, Prahran. The hand coming out to take the money was supposed to be Gudinski's I think.

There wasn't so much cross-pollination with other cultures back then, and that's why the music scene flourished, there was no internet, no VCR's, if you wanted entertainment you had to go out and be with people. Everything was very local, Skyhooks big ambition was to make it in Sydney, perhaps I should've aimed a bit higher! It seemed an impossibility to crack Sydney, but we did it, with a bit of help from Double J, as it was called then. My perception was that the sharpie thing wasn't as strong in Sydney, mostly Melbourne and to a certain extent Adelaide. I'd say sharpie started to fade when we were rising to prominence, by '77 it was definitely fading, Lobby Loyde and Buster Brown were gone, there just didn't seem to be the bands around anymore."

4

1976
- 80

Bob
"I was in Turana about thirty-six times, the wardens suggested I should have my own keys so I could come and go as I pleased. First time I went in there were ten or twenty sharps in there. The next time it was more like a hundred, same blokes, they'd all just been converted. When I got out, mid '75, things were coming to a halt."

By 1976 sharpies second golden age was all but over. There were still scores of gangs out there, but it was nothing like the Everest peak of '73/74. Most of the top sharp bands had thrown in the towel, or were trying to make it big overseas, and the live scene was left most dull by their departure.

Then came the Tatts. With the exception of Mick Cocks, Rose Tattoo's personnel had all spent the early seventies playing in blues/hard-rock bands- Peter Wells in Buffalo, Ian Rilen in Band of Light, Angry Anderson, Digger Royal and later Geordie Leach in Buster Brown. Each of those bands contained a germ of Rose Tattoo's greatness, but the combination of Anderson/Wells/Rilen/Cocks/Royal- a fraternity of blitzkrieg if ever there was one- threw them well into the shade. Rose Tattoo were simply the most dynamic Oz-rock band this side of the Coloured Balls.

What with Angry having entertained the troops with Buster back in the cult's heyday, any band he fronted was going to attract a sharp audience, even if it was just for old times sake. So when the sharp kids caught a whiff of what kind of outfit the Tatts were, flat-out rockin' and street-steeped in the absolute, there was no keeping them away. By all accounts Buster Brown could really slay 'em live, but it must be said that on disc they're merely so-so. Rosey Tatts on the other hand, were startling. For sheer purity of vision Rose Tattoo's self titled debut is untouchable. Some might turn thumbs down at said vision, it's certainly not pretty, but its impact is undeniable- the most full-throttle collection of Oz-rock ever pressed into disc.

ANGRY ANDERSON

"I started out as a rocker, brushback rocker, sideburns, black clothes, white socks, the '56 rocker style- we wanted to look like Crash Craddock, Elvis. In my heart of hearts I'm still a rocker. The first guys that I can remember cutting their hair short had what they called a college cut, they called themselves '64 rockers. I'm a person who's into symmetry, some might say anally, and I thought that if they waited one more year '65/56 would've been the exact reverse- numerically speaking that might've been quite a magical statement.

I was never one of the City Sharps, but I identified with them. I was one of the early long hair kids, the English look, the Beatles. In Coburg, where I grew up, there were very few long-haired mod kids. In those early sharpie days I was caught between identifying very strongly with my area- the kids I went to school with, many of whom ended up full-fledged gang members- and the influence of music. Saturday afternoon we'd go to the local ground to watch the football and the guys would ask me what I was doing that night and as often as not I'd be going to a jazz or blues club, Frank Kramer's, places like that. My uncle Ivan was a big influence on me, got me into music, he was-still is- a jazz drummer, he's got his own swing band to this day. Swing music very quickly introduces you to other kinds of black music, boogie, blues- so it was a natural progression and I got heavily into the blues. I remember an ex-girlfriend asked me what I was going to do with my life and I told her I was going to be a blues singer, that was my main thing. All the bands I've been in were definitely blues based. Rose Tatts were a blues band, everything we wrote was modern day blues- we just played fast rather than plodding.

Sharps wore a lot of the same clothing as English mods- the first time I saw a three-button shirt, a crest-knit, was on Roger Daltrey or someone like that. Twin-sets were huge, the matching crest-knit and cardigan- maroon, silver grey, royal blue or chocolate brown- I remember guys who'd only wear one colour or had complete outfits in one colour. Some areas would claim a colour was theirs. Some guys even had their cars painted- EH and EJ's were the absolute. In recent years I've tried to re-adopt the look, but it's very hard to find a twin-set for a guy! I went into storage and the only item of clothing I had left was my Bokka coat, three-quarter length, flap pockets, hounds-tooth black, white and grey- I can barely get it on.

Preston boys were pretty formidable, Box Hill was strong, Richmond, Essendon, North Melbourne, Brunswick, Fawkner, Collingwood boys were revered- for sheer ferocity they were it. Broadmeadows was always a problem for us in Coburg. We all worked in the local factories, as did a lot of British migrant girls- English, Scottish, Irish- and a lot of them lived in housing commission places in Broady. We'd go up there, they liked our company, but we had a lot of trouble with the Broadmeadows boys, I can't remember ever getting along with them in those years. We really didn't have an awful lot to do with far-flung areas, certainly not your middle class/upper middle class neighbourhoods. If you came from a working class area you didn't often move out of that area, although music used to take me to the city. The difference between working class and middle class was, in those days, quite distinct. It struck me as curious finding out later that sharp had taken such a strong hold on middle class areas, but it did, because it was a machismo/boy thing.

If the local law caught you out on the street too many times they'd say 'Let's see a bit more of you down the gym', as a way of trying to get you to use up your energy in a more positive way, and to get to know you. The gyms were in Collingwood, Richmond, Fitzroy- the places where most boxers grew up. A lot of the top fellas would train in the gyms.

In those days people used to talk about ' good form'. To have 'good form' meant you didn't fight with anything but your hands, and some guys were that good that they could always settle things with their fists. Weapons- bars and hammers, came into it in gang confrontations when you felt you had to make up for lack of numbers or whatever. Later on 'good form' meant that your gang was strong, was feared. Being a top fella wasn't about thuggery, to be a top fella you had to be strong, capable, fair- and you had to be a friendly likeable bloke, all the qualities boys are going to look for in a leader. At the bottom of the hierarchy were 'Apprentices'- you put in a certain amount of time to earn your badge if you like, there's a Buster Brown song of that name and that's essentially what it's about.

Buster Brown was a chance to re-live. I'd realized by then what a significant era sharp had been. The thing that always struck me was that it was uniquely Australian, uniquely Melbourne- although eventually working class kids all around the country locked onto it and claimed it as their own. It was such a flamboyant and extravagant thing to happen.

In Buster I wanted to make sure that the street-tough attitude of the music was expressed in the image as well, so I started to affect the old look and cut my hair short. In their early days Buster didn't really have a direction. I wouldn't say I was responsible for the direction of the band but when a singer has a certain image and stance it influences the band. We decided we'd be a real 'street' band, the voice of the kids. Phil Rudd also gave the band that image, that edge- Phil was tattooed, was from the same sort of background as me and had a bit of grunt to him. It was strange in the Buster days to look out at the crowd and see this whole new generation of sharps- it had become a tradition, although by that time it had become something new because the English skinhead thing had come along. You couldn't help but accommodate that skinhead influence- it was too similar for it not to affect things and it was absorbed very quickly.

One of my best friends, one of the great 'Top Fellas' is a guy from Adelaide called Oscar. When we used to go to Adelaide with Buster, and later Tatts, Oscar and the Adelaide sharps would just get me into so much trouble, I had some fantastic times with them. They were infamous throughout Adelaide, they stood up to the cops on several occasions, stood up against baton charges, dogs- real last ditch outlaw stand. Buster played Adelaide on a bill with the Aztecs and the Coloured Balls- talk about a recipe for mayhem- huge blues, they came in from all over and beat the shit out of each other.

Buster played very few inner-city gigs, we'd mostly play out in the suburbs, places like Q-Club, which was the sharp stronghold, the mecca. We only started playing the city venues- Sebastian's and places like that, when we became so popular that they couldn't afford not to book us. There was nothing wrong with

Buster in its day but I think if I'd have been able to form Rose Tattoo at the time I would've- there just weren't that many guys around who wanted to do it.

When the Tatts started in '76 we pulled a lot of sharps and skinheads out of the woodwork. When Tattoo came along the whole thing was receding. Bill was gone, Lob was gone and they didn't really have a band. When we went to Melbourne in those early days we had guys coming out we hadn't seen for years saying 'We've got a band again'. It was a winning thing for me, it made me feel, I don't know, like we'd proved something.

The song that really captures the sharp era is 'Butcher and Fast Eddie'. Butcher was an actual person, we made up the name 'Fast Eddie' because we didn't know the other guy's name. Butcher was from Coburg, I didn't know him but I knew of him, Eddie was from either Beaumaris or Frankston. From what I can tell Butcher is in jail, has been in and out of jail for most of his life, and is going to be there for a long time. I've had people ask me if I'm Butcher! No, not likely.

I don't think there were too many people killed in those days, the mid sixties, but there were a few. I've been told of a mass blue at a party where a guy was kicked to death, and I remember hearing a story about how one, possibly two, blokes were beaten to death behind Broady Town Hall, which used to hold a dance called The White Elephant. There were some ferocious fights there, dozens and dozens of blokes. I only went there a couple of times, and I have to tell you, I only went because a lot of our fellas were going, I didn't like the atmosphere, really tense.

I think the Coloured Balls were probably one of the greatest rock bands ever and it was difficult for me when Lobby came to play with the Tatts and chose to play bass, rather than guitar. I'd waited years to be in a band with Lobby on guitar. When the Balls and Buster broke up, Digger and I played with Lobby, Bobsie and John Miglans for a couple of months. I kind of thought that would become a band, there was talk about writing songs, but it didn't last.

I don't think he'd remember, but I first met Lobby when he was playing in the Purple Hearts. It was the first time I'd ever seen him play and he was just the best. I went up to him after the gig and told him what a great player I thought he was. I saw Lobby go through a couple of bands, the Hearts, the Wild Cherries. I'd always go and see them and I guess I became a familiar face in the crowd and he'd always say g'day when he saw me. A few years later I was in Buster and we became friends. Lobby more than anybody got me obsessed with loud music. Lobby always played loud, that was one of the most striking things about him. He had so much attack in his playing, a desperation, an urgency- and that, to me, was rock n' roll. There were a lot of great guitarists at the time who I thought were just the duck's guts as players, but there's only one Lobby.

Going to England with the Tatts in the Early Eighties we saw the skinhead thing full tilt. Garry Bushell from 'Sounds' really had a thing for the band, he identified very strongly with us, he knew instinctively what drove the band, what made us more than just a loud rock n' roll band. He was a big Oi! boy, when I first met him he had the boots, military trousers, short hair and braces- he looked like a London skinhead. He and I got to be good pals at the time. He came on tour with us and introduced us to a lot of Oi! and ska bands. He took us to see bands that have since become legendary- Sham, Cockney Rejects- and a lot of them were short-haired, tattooed guys from working class backgrounds. The first time I ever met Wattie from the Exploited was with Gary- I spent a whole night listening to him talk and didn't understand a word he said!

From the start Rilen had a thing about punk, not wanting to copy it, Rilen's definitely an original, but to play with that intensity, that edge. I've got a book at home on Aussie rock and there's a section in there on Punk- Bill's in it, Lobby's in it and Rose Tatts are in it. We were punks in the same way that Gene Vincent, Eddie Cochran and Marlon Brando were punks."

1976 saw the birth of the Sex Pistols, a birth accompanied by enough hype and headlines to sink the Bismarck, or indeed, the Queen Mary. The whole Sex Pistols tale has been told so many times now that it's become a bore, there's been way too much ink spilt on the subject, most of it pretentious blather, for me to bother throwing in my two cents. I've got better things to do with my money. Suffice to say they were the biggest showstopper in rock since the Beatles.

Sharpies, always quick to catch onto the latest developments in British rock, went into varying degrees of ecstasy over the Sex Pistols. They offered a full dose of what the glam groups had but flirted with- raw power rock n' roll, no frills, no beg your parsnips. And then there was the image, the glam delinquent togs, the dead-end sneers, what could be more sharpie than that? Sharps identified with the Pistols in the same way they identified with AC/DC, they felt the band were of them and spoke for them. Indeed it's generally forgotten that, in their early days, AC/DC were often labelled a punk band themselves. This was before the Pistols and the British punk outburst, back when the tag was hung on anyone who played it simple and snotty.

Sharpies dug the Pistols as a killer new rock group, no different to Slade or Alice Cooper. When punk emerged as a movement, a new youth cult with strict fashion codes and a hard line on breaking with the past, the sharp world was divided.

Mick

"I was a sharp from '76 till '80 when I started hanging around the Ballroom, it was a lot more sedate, more music orientated. There were quite a lot of ex-sharps in the punk scene, a lot of girls, some of the better people. Most sharps liked the Pistols, they could identify with the urban nihilism, but initially a lot of sharps were hostile to punk, because it was outside our culture."

The Crystal Ballroom opened in '79 and quickly became the focal point of Melbourne's punk/new wave scene. Located on Fitzroy Street, St Kilda, the Ballroom was just down the road from the Esplanade and popular sharpie nightspots like Mickey's, Bananas and Kingston Rock. It wasn't long before sharpies started turning up at the Ballroom, some curious about the new music, others with more malevolent intentions.

Bill

"For me, sharpie died when punk happened. Punk was exciting it had more meaning. About ten or fifteen of us started going to the Ballroom and that was good, but eventually we'd get kicked out because the stupid ones had to leave their mark and started fighting and carrying on. They weren't prepared to move on and try and get along with these people, university kids from well off families. But a few of us kept going and got away with it, by this stage we still had the haircuts and would occasionally wear Connys but the clothes were changing because we didn't want to get into fights, we wanted to get into clubs."

There were essentially three sharpie responses to punk. Some remained totally antagonistic to it, roughing up any punks unlucky enough to cross their path. Others dived in boots n' all, dropping the sharp image and throwing their lot in with the Ballroom crowd. A greater number hedged their bets. They still wore their Connys and ran in mobs, but they'd sometimes hang around the punk clubs and got into a bit of the punk music and fashion.

By the second half of the seventies, after years of bad press and bad behaviour, being a sharpie had become downright hazardous to your health. Step out your front door in sharp garb and people would start queuing up to take you on. Battle-fatigue pervaded.

Bill

"By that stage we had a bad reputation, it wasn't just a fashion, it was kill or be killed. Every time we went out you'd end up running from someone or beat-

ing someone up. It wasn't me and I got sick of it."

Mick
"Sharpies never made themselves too popular, they sort of got hassled out of existence."

Most of the kids that jumped ship from sharp to punk were coming to the end of their teens and were no longer so hung up on being the toughest guy that ever breathed. They wanted out of the gang scene but didn't necessarily want to retire to Squaresville. Punk was as exciting and rebellious as sharpie, with the same kind of lively music and fashion scene, but its energy was all creative. Punks weren't so prone to thumping each other.

Punk swallowed up a lot of the second-generation sharpies in the same way hippie had with the Sixties originals. Both offered rebellion without blood and with a social conscience/political agenda, however ill-defined. A lot of ex-sharps ended up big wheels in the punk scene, a fact that's rarely acknowledged.

Most accounts of punk Melbourne concentrate on Nick Cave, the Boys Next Door and the art/angst/smack brigade. Myself, I've never rated

Cave. For one thing, his music's shithouse. For two things, he's a pseud, double distilled. For my money the most interesting group to come out of the Melbourne punk scene were La Femme, the only local punk band to fully win over the sharpie audience.

La Femme were ex-sharps themselves, an interesting parallel with the Sex Pistols (Steve Jones, Paul Cook and Glen Matlock were all skinheads in their early teens). 'Chelsea Kids' La Femme's 45 debut was a real stormer, a chunky glam/punk rave-up, all nadsat lyrics and dewy eyed reminiscence of a youth spent punching-on with the Bayside sharps (the Chelsea kids of the title). La Femme were glam babies, their sound was shaped by Bowie, Slade and Sweet as much as it was by the Pistols, Clash and Damned (all of whom pinched a move or two from glam themselves). Never content to stay inside the insular St Kilda punk world, La Femme took their music to every inner-city rock venue and far-flung suburban pub that would have them. It paid off. With their high-energy performances and glam-metallic sound they won over the pub-rock audience in a way that faux-weirdies like Cave's mob never could. Typically, the pseud-set snubbed them. They played rock n' roll at a time when everyone else was coming on arty, and they weren't afraid to court the mass-pop audience.

CHANE CHANE

"I left school when I was 14 and got a job on the wharf, loading containers. I used to go into the city on the weekend with friends from my area and one week I went in wearing make-up, red, white and blue stripes. One of the Melbourne skinheads, he had the t-shirt, came up and called me a poof, I told him to get fucked. I thought I'd get my head punched in but I knew I'd make a good fight of it, I'd been learning martial arts since I was eleven. His girlfriend stepped in, thought I had balls, and I started knocking around with them. The girl, Helen, popped up years later at the Ballroom, a big person on the punk scene. I thought hanging out with the Melbourne skins was prestige. I'd been to see Slade at the Melbourne showgrounds and there was a great load of skinheads there. They wore Doc Marten boots and t-shirts or rugby collared tops with the sleeves cut off. I saw them attack these other guys with bottles, knives, chains, I thought, that's a show of force, that's power.

Melbourne skins didn't have too many organised fights, it was mostly just going around town hassling people. I was like a little mascot to these guys, who were eighteen and older. They'd send me up to a group of guys and I'd say 'My brothers told me to ask you for money' they'd say 'Fuck off kid' and I'd say 'Look behind you', and they'd all be there, shaved heads, tattoos on their necks.

I was with them for a while but then some guy in jail ordered me dead, I don't know what it was about, something stupid.

A whole lot of the main core of the Melbourne skins went to jail and a lot of new people came in. That was the start of the Melbourne Sharps. Sharps were into fashion, you had to be working because you spent a lot of money, everything tailored. You had to drink like a fish and fight like five guys, real blokey. We thought we were quite natural, you could have tatoos and an earring but that was about it, you couldn't wear a ring through your nose or anything hippyish. We were like a hangover from the Menzies era.

We used to follow the football a lot. A lot of the sharpie sheilas were hair-dressers and they'd hang around with a lot of gay guys because most hair-dressers at the time were gay, a stereotype but true. These guys were mixed up with the Collingwood cheer-squad, which had a lot of gay guys in it. So we'd all go to Vic Park and hang around with the cheer-squad and if anyone had a go at them, we'd fix them up.

I left Melbourne sharps and started a gang in Ascot vale. I was the leader because I had a bit of a reputation in the sharpie world. We used to just cause mayhem, I remember shoving guns through people's windows, crazy stuff.

Then we got invited to Glenroy. There was a big gang up there called the A.N.As. I think A.N.A stood for Australian National Airways or something like that. There was an estate up there owned by Reg Ansett, and every street name in the area ended with 'ana', there's Tarana, Dromana, Kadana etc. Three of us got invited to one of their barbecues, big bonfire in a paddock. They ended up choosing me but not the other two guys: they threw them off a cliff, which kind of ended my friendship with them.

A lot of people had left Melbourne sharps and joined other groups because there was a lot of in fighting and back stabbing, the suburban gangs were more unified. A lot of my friends from Melbourne sharps ended up in a Fawkner gang called Anderson Road Sharps, their headquarters was the Fawkner cemetery. I thought that was really cool- come visit us, you won't be leaving.

The thing I didn't like about sharpies was that most of the time you'd be fighting other sharpie gangs. I couldn't see the sense in that, they were just like us, they liked the same things. If we'd got to know each other we probably would've been the best of friends.

A gang of guys onto one was considered uncool. We always fought evenly. If one guy wanted to fight me, fair enough, it's me against him, which was stupid enough because we didn't know each other- we were only fighting because we were from different sides of town. It was kind of like football, you had your club

and you played with your club, and you didn't transfer either!

The A.N.As versus the Bayside Sharps was an interesting war.

The Bayside guys used to go to the football at Essendon. One day we waited for them in the subway at Essendon Station, we had it full of guys, baseball bats and everything. The football finished and none of us had really thought it through, we thought it would be just Bayside Sharps coming down, but of course there was about 10,000 other people as well. But when they did come along we thought, fuck it, and charged them anyway. There was about forty of them but only ten or so came at us. We laid them out, real kung fu movie stuff. The rest of the crowd thought they were caught in a riot, started throwing punches and freaking out, an all in brawl, seemed like a thousand people fighting and the rest trying to get past them. I dived onto a bus and I've got a big piece of wood in my hands that's dripping with blood. I tell the bus driver to go, he wont go. I threaten him, he says he can't go people have got to get the bus. I point to the Bayside Sharps who are running for the bus and tell him 'They're going to kill me and they'll probably kill you too'. He goes.

One day I was waiting for my girlfriend at Moonee Ponds Station when a train pulls up and there's two carriages full of Bayside Sharps.

I ran towards the pizza place opposite the station with sixty to eighty guys chasing after me. I made it just near the doorway, got king-hit from behind and hit the ground. I'm rolled up on the floor and I hear this clanging- the guys from the pizza shop were helping me, smacking them on the head with pizza trays, chasing them off. So I get away but I'm angry, I go up to Puckle Street, to a billiard hall, the sharpies who hung out at billiard halls were always gunnies, they were older, they sold drugs, and there was always a gun around. There was a guy I knew from the early Melbourne sharp days up there, Blackie. We got some guys, got a car, but they'd scattered. I got a broken nose and a broken cheek out of that, spent a night in hospital. My girlfriend called me at the hospital, one of the Bayside Sharps had called her. They said they'd been getting a lot of heat for belting me, two of their guys had been shot already, not dead, and a few had been belted, so they wanted to work out some kind of truce. We decide that they'd send a couple of their guys to hang around with us for a night and vice versa, so we could get to know and understand each other. Our guys were given girls and beer and had a good time, we took their guys to the most dangerous places we could go. Took them down to High Point West and nearly got into a fight with a hundred of the Footscray guys, the Bayside guys thought we were nuts, and we were, we didn't give a fuck, we thought we'd be sharpies forever.

After the A.N.As I started a Clockwork Orange inspired gang called Oak Park Boot Boys. I've got dyslexia, I taught myself to read so I could learn Nadsat. I read 'A Clockwork Orange' and 'Skinhead'. Oak Park Boot Boys was a couple of the A.N.As, a couple of people from the West Road Sharps, and a few others from Oak Park who we picked because they were gigantic and tough. I just said 'You're a monster, you've got to come in with us'. We dressed up Clockwork Orange style, went out at midnight and caused mayhem till the early hours of the morning. I don't know how I did it because I had to be at work at seven thirty a.m, but I did it, for years.

When I was a skinhead I hated drugs, anyone who used drugs I would spit on them. But when we got into the Clockwork Orange thing we started doing acid because it was really bizarre to fight on acid, everything in slow motion.

I was knocking around with this English skinhead who'd been living in Adelaide. He'd moved to Melbourne and saw the Oak Park Bootboys in the city and started hanging around with us. He came over to my place one day and he brought over a record someone had just sent him from England. It was 'Anarchy in the U.K', about a year before it came out here. I loved it. I thought, this is new, this is different. I'd always liked things with a bit of attitude, so punk was perfect. We evolved into the punk thing. We'd be standing in front of the shops, group of sharpies, but we'd have safety pins in our ears, dressing a bit like punks.

One night around this time I went out with some mates and when I got back to my house I noticed someone looking through the blinds. I opened the door, and there he is, the guy from Melbourne Skins who'd been in jail and wanted to kill me. I was shitting myself, he had about twenty guys with him, three of them had shotguns, two with pistols. I just thought fast and started poking him in the chest, telling him we'll go outside and fight to the death. So we go outside and ZOOM, I'm gone, I flew away. I'd left home when I was 14, but I went back to my parent's house for a while because I had nowhere else to go, I had to get out of that flat right away. There were a couple of weeks there after that where I didn't give a fuck about my life. If I'd found him, I'd have killed him.

But then Peter and Graham asked me to join them in a band. I'd won a few dancing competitions at sharpie dances so they knew I had enough front. La Femme started from there and that was the end of sharpie for me, I'd had enough, this was '76. Peter and Graham had been in the A.N.A.'s and they'd played in Teenage Radio Stars with James Freud and Sean Kelly, but they couldn't put up with those guys and their attitudes. We got in another A.N.A guy on guitar but he didn't work out so we held auditions and found Brett and he was perfect. In '77 we recorded 'Chelsea Kids' at the TCS studios round the back of Channel 9, Missing Link put it out first and RCA picked it up later. We got a manager to come and see us in rehearsal, he signed us up and six months later we're on Countdown. It happened really quickly for us, we were the right thing at the right time, we were one of the few punk bands playing it really hard back then. We did a couple of gigs with the Boys Next Door, they had their arty-farty thing going. We did about

four weeks with them, we'd headline one week and they'd headline the next and so on. On the second week we were playing the Ballroom, we're rehearsing and they walk in, noses in the air, giggling. We thought, fuck these guys, dropped our instruments, jumped off stage and started punching into them. We had three of them crying. We thought, these guys aren't punks, they're just playing punk, weekend punks.

We didn't like most of the other bands, they hadn't been through what we'd been through. Punk was the first thing they'd ever done, whereas we'd settled down into punk to reminisce about our crazy days.

The morning after we played Countdown I had to go from Elwood to Thomastown where I was working as a painter. After work, waiting at the train station all these school girls recognised me, I thought what the fuck? Oh yeah, I was on television last night. We were the first band ever to do Countdown without a record. We didn't even have a deal.

Occasionally the sharpie in us would come out. We used to play at the Champion Hotel a lot. This was before it became a big punk venue- that was upstairs- we used to play downstairs to an audience of wharfies and Aboriginals.

The bass player from Real Life told me that he spat at me when I was on stage at the Champion, as people did, and I jumped off and punched his head in. I must have been a little crazed that night. He was very nice about it later.

Graham had a fat bodied Fender and smacked it into a guy's face who was going to hit his girlfriend with a bottle. For a while we had a guy called Rod on drums, he was the bouncer at Croxton Park, big reputation. He was filling in because Peter was in jail. He was in for something he'd done years earlier, as a sharpie, and it just caught up with him.

We were a live band, the records and the TV wasn't so important to us. I just liked singing and being able to voice my ideas. Back then this country was very uptight, had a stick up its ass. I think our generation pulled it out a bit, we certainly got a lot of shit on us. Subsequently Australia's got a little more funk in its walk now."

If you were a sharpie and plugged in to punk, Sham 69 were irresistible. Sham got together in 1977 and quickly became one of the biggest punk groups in Britain. Sham's beefy pub-punk sound was nothing new, but they had tons of passion, catchy rabble rousing tunes and in Jimmy Pursey, a front-man who could not be denied. They also had a rabid following of thousands of skinheads, 'The Sham Army'.

A British skinhead revival had been brewing since '75. It was a football thing. There was a feeling amongst the kids that terrace fashion had gotten a little too shaggy, that it was time to go back to basics. The same feeling that had produced punk. The first groups to win over the new skinhead audience were Cocksparrer and Slaughter and the Dogs, proto-punk groups in a glam/Faces bag. Skinheads who may have been suspicious of what they perceived as the art school posing of punk, found a door into the new music via straight-down-the-line street-rock groups like Slaughter, Cocksparrer and later Menace, Skrewdriver and of course Sham. The post-punk skinheads stripped the '69 look to its bare essentials:

D.M's, denims, braces, t-shirts. Punk had upped the ante in the scaring the citizens stakes so a lot of kids went for a more extreme look- zero crops, bigger boots (fourteen holers!) and facial tats. Not all the new skins wanted to look quite so mental, and many dug into the more dapper corners of the old skin wardrobe, the harrington/sta-prest/button-down side of things.

The skinhead revival grew with Sham's success. By '78 Sham were bonafide chart dwellers and skinheads were back on a grand scale. But all was far from apples. The Sham Army were loyal, but a wee bit too lively. Any time the band played they were confronted with scores of skins, punks and soccer hooligans, all hell bent on not sorting out their differences like civilised gents. This situation pushed the band into quasi-retirement, fearful of playing live lest more blood be spilled. I'm sure that Lobby Loyde, living in London at the time, felt no end of sympathy for the band. But the troublemakers at Sham gigs were a little different to the old Q-Club crowd. A portion of Sham's skinhead following were supporters of the extreme right National Front. They sieg-heiled the band and passed out racist pamphlets at their gigs. The band in no way approved of such doings but short of having everyone tied and muzzled as they entered the gig there was little they could do about it. By '78/79 Sham concerts were seen as a great place to get yourself half-murdered and the band had little choice but to call it quits.

With Sham gone their skinhead following latched onto new groups like the Cockney Rejects, the Angelic Upstarts, Madness and the Specials. The NF element were snapped up by Skrewdriver, who gradually deteriorated from the great Stonesy punk band of their first album 'All Skrewed Up', into an awful plod-metal band with a race-hate agenda.

The British skinhead revival had a big impact on Melbourne sharpie kids.

Mick
"By '78/79 you had bands like Sham 69 and the resurgence of English skinhead. You had gangs like the Murrumbeena Skins, they called themselves skinheads rather than sharps, they dressed pretty much the same but they were more inclined to wear D.M's and listen to the new English groups."

At the same time there were younger kids coming up who aped the new British skinhead style with no sharpie influence, they didn't wear Connys, they didn't listen to Lobby Loyde, they were strictly post-punk Anglophile. In '79 these kids were a tiny minority but their numbers grew as sharpies ebbed. One of Melbourne's first post-punk skinhead crews were the Bayswater Skins, a mob that were spoken of with considerable reverence when I was serving my time as a skinhead, in the latter half of the eighties.

Sammy
"In the late seventies there were only about a dozen English style skinheads, but they were ultra hard. The Bayswater Skins got into a fight with the Westside Sharps around this time."

Westside Sharps versus Bayswater skins was a run of the mill gang-clash of the kind that both teams would've engaged in at regular intervals. And yet in another way, it was a truly epochal confrontation, a battle between the future (Bayswater) and the past (Westside). Regardless of who walked away the victor on the day, the ultimate winner was obvious. The new skinheads were on the ascendant and sharpies' days were numbered.

By the time punk came along the glam bands were pretty much dead and buried, but Bowie endured. Around '77 there was even a thirty strong crew called the Melbourne Bowies, they came and went as quickly as you like, but their mere existence is testament to the hold the man had on the sharp set.

On the night before Bowie's '79 concert at the Melbourne Cricket Ground there was a bit of a one sided donnybrook that a lot of people remember. The papers ran it big and it was later to inspire a scene in Richard Lowenstein's film 'Dogs in Space' ('86). A large number of dedicated Bowie adorers spent the night camping for tickets outside the grounds. Around

midnight a mob of about a dozen Westside and ex-Melbourne Sharps crashed the scene and launched an attack on some kids who by all accounts did nothing to earn their antipathy. One poor bugger copped a beer bottle in the face.

In defence of sharpie kind it must be said that there were plenty of sharps in the crowd that night that perpetrated no such villainies, and were simply waiting in line like everyone else.

The support group at the Bowie concert were the Angels, climbing the rungs at the time thanks to hit 45's like 'Am I Ever Gonna See Your Face Again' and 'Take a Long Line'. The 'Alberts' triumvirate of the Tatts, Seedies and Angels were the boss sharp bands of the cult's final days. The Angels mixed old-time seventies hard rock/rhythm-and-blues with new wave punch and directness, and thus were a sure-fire hit with the new punk/sharp crossover audience. They became, of course, one of the champeen Oz-rock groups of the eighties, but for me, good as they were, they lacked the wallop of their more raw-knuckled peers.

Sharpies are depicted in several Australian films. 'Dogs in Space' and 'Eight Ball' feature brief 'go for a cuppa and you'll miss it' scenes of sharpies. Or so I'm told, I haven't actually seen either of them. Sorry. Both are retrospective representations made long after the cult's demise. A carload of sharpies attempt to run the junkie heroes of Bert Deling's brilliant 'Pure Shit' ('77) off the road. 'Hard Knocks' ('80) stars Tracy Mann as a delinquent street kid trying to make good. In the first half of the film Mann sports a sharpie haircut and semi-sharp threads. She's not decked out in the full sharp fashion, truth be told she's a bit of a scruff, but then by 1980 unemployment was on the rise, and things were much bleaker for working class youth than they had been five years earlier. A lot of kids drawn to sharp in the late Seventies and early eighties lacked the money for tailored threads. Many were homeless and involved in petty crime. Smack and glue sniffing were also a growing problem. Homeless junkies don't tend to be the snazziest dressers, so I'd say Mann's look is pretty right for the time.

1979 saw 'The Warriors' take a place alongside 'A Clockwork Orange' and the kung fu films in the pantheon of movies most loved by the sharps. The Warriors was director Walter Hill's juiced-up riff on Sol Yurick's 1965 novel of the same name, itself a riff on 'Anabasis' by Xenophon. The film is set in a fantasy New York where teen gangs in rock star fancy dress battle it out while Civvy Street slumbers. It was totally in sync with the sharps' macho-romantic view of themselves.

In the latter half of the seventies the sharpie rig-out was modified in various ways. Flares and platforms were thrown over in favour of straight-legged jeans and flat-heeled shoes or Cubans. Miller shirts were also nixed. Black leather jackets came in (tight and cropped with long pointed collars), as did sleeveless Saba t-shirts (black or white), Adidas Romes and striped silk-weave polo tops. You could still get a Conny made to order but less finicky customers could now get them off the rack at Myers or men's stores like Adam's.

By '77 the sharp gangland was in low tide. Back in the cult's glory days forming a mob was as easy as eating your breakfast. Most fighting lads were sharpies and it was simply a matter of rounding up the local talent. Alternately, you could throw your lot in with Melbourne Sharps. But Melbourne Sharps expired around '76, and new recruits to the cult were a lot less bountiful. It was a time of amalgamation, of units from different neighbourhoods joining forces to up their numbers.

Mick
"I got into sharpie in my mid teens, around '76. I was from Oakleigh and there were a few of us about. A lot of the Hughesdale boys at the time were sharps and there'd been sharp gangs in South Oakleigh, Clayton and Holmesglen. I was in Westside Sharps for a while. They started in early '78 and lasted about two years. They had a core of about twelve people, six guys and six

girls. They were made up of two groups that got together, one lot from Footscray, Sunshine and St Albans, the other from Oakleigh, Dandenong, Cranbourne and Ashburton. Because we came from both sides of the city we'd meet at Flinders Street Station. Melbourne Sharps had finished by then. We'd also hang around Chadstone Bowls with the Holmesglen Skins. In '78 Westside absorbed St Albans Sharps and Newland Sharps, six guys from Coburg and five girls from Ferntree Gully. Vic Sharps- Victorian Sharps, were a breakaway group from Westside. After I left Westside in early '79 I was in Southside Sharps which was focused around Clayton and was a coming together of sharps from Moorabin, Jordanville, Oakleigh, Clayton and Elsternwick. They lasted about six months. A few years later there was an attempt to start it up again with different guys. When Southside started to fragment a few of us started hanging around Geelong a bit, with the Geelong Sharps. They had a core of Yugoslavian guys. Sharps and Co were a gang made up of Geelong and Malvern Sharps who hung around East Malvern sniffing glue. Eastside Sharps came out of the Northside Boys, a gang from the South-East suburbs made up of sharps and non-sharps. Malvern Sharps became Central Sharps with people from Geelong, Thomastown and Footscray.

There was also the Frankston sharps, Dandenong sharps and Doveton Skins. Thomastown Sharps had a real tight pecking order. They'd walk in two's, long line, and if you were going to walk with them you could walk down the end of the line."

Bill

"At the time there would've been a thousand or more sharps in Melbourne. Thomastown were the biggest, toughest gang. Country guys and built like it, huge."

Everybody remembers the 1979 Lalor car park shoot-em-up between the Thomastown Sharps and the Reservoir Boys, it's probably the most oft-told war story in the annals of sharp. Five blokes were shot and sixteen were charged with everything from GBH to starting a riot. It made all the papers and consolidated Thomastown's reputation as the heaviest gang of the day. But the fact is it never happened, not the way the papers told it anyway. I know because I went right to the source, John Bow AKA Bowie, one-time leader of the Thomastown sharps.

JOHN BOW

"I hit the streets when I was about twelve, started hanging around the espresso bars and billiard halls. When I was at Thomastown High, 1974, Reservoir Lakeside High came down to play us at football. Our team were mostly long-hairs and Reservoir were all sharps. As soon as the game started they were punching on, the teachers had to stop the game. One of the first sharps I knew was a Greek guy called Big Jim, body builder, always with a girl on each arm. Nobody messed with him. I first got a sharpie haircut when I was about fifteen. I started hanging around with the Melbourne Sharps, then I got a bit pissed off with them. This was near their last days, in the early seventies they were tough guys, but by '76 they were pretty piss-weak, I thought a lot of them were cowards. So I went back to Thomastown and we started a gang, only three of us to start with, but we got into a few fights, our numbers grew, and we were going from about '76 to '82. We weren't really in it for the fashion, we were in it for the violence. We had nothing better to do. We wanted to be the number one gang in Melbourne and we were, the biggest and probably the most violent. We took it very seriously. Our motto was 'one in, all in', it wasn't fair but that's the way it was.

We'd go into the local pizza shop and the owners would give us free pizzas so that we'd go away. They knew that if any drunks came in from the pub and had a go, we'd punch the shit out of them and the shop would get wrecked. It happened so many times.

I had to keep the peace. Once I went to Mildura, I came back and the gang had split in two. It was Blackie and Murray, the two toughest guys in Thomastown, hated by everybody in Melbourne. They'd fight three times a week, smash each other with bottles- they split the group. I got them back together, you had to get them fighting other people so they wouldn't fight among themselves.

The fighting with the Reservoir boys started because a few of our boys gave a guy from Reservoir a bad belting on a train one night. Later that night a few car loads of Reservoir boys came to Thomastown and chased a few of our blokes. Then one of them tried to get on with one of my girlfriends and I wasn't too happy about that. A few of us gave him a belting, more fuel to the fire. They were saying they were gonna do this and they were gonna do that but they weren't doing nothing. About seven of us walked through Reservoir one night, through the shops where they used to hang out. The word got around that we were coming and there was about eight carloads of them. We just walked through and they did nothing. We thought it was a bit of a joke, thought they didn't have much guts.

There was a place in Reservoir called Scab's Alley. It was a paddock next door to the drive-in. We'd go up there on the weekend with some girls, jump the fence and turn the speakers up. There was a load of old car seats there and we'd sit and watch the movies. About sixteen of our guys went down there one night and on the way home, about one in the morning, they saw two cars full of Reservoir Boys, parked outside the shops where we used to hang out at. They ran at the Reservoir Boys to give them a hiding, but the Reservoir Boys pulled out shotguns and started firing and they had to back off. Things were getting serious.

One night about five of us were at the shops and someone came flying down the road. He was a guy from Reservoir who'd come to warn us that there were eight carloads of Reservoir Boys coming. We took off. We decided we had to do something about this, but we had to get reinforcements and we had to get guns. We wanted to put them out of action, it'd been going on too long.

My mate Louie, a Yugoslavian guy, suggested we go down to Footscray, he knew some big Yugos from there and they had guns. We rounded up all the guys we could find in Footscray, but when we got back to Reservoir we couldn't find anyone. If we'd got hold of Reservoir that night we'd have shot them so it's lucky we didn't. This was the night of the shooting. The Reservoir boys had come for us, we'd gone to Footscray, then they'd gone to Lalor and had a shoot out with these other guys, Italian and Greek guys who were our enemies too. Obviously they'd been looking for us, couldn't find us, felt like a fight with someone, gone to Lalor, shot at Lalor, who have then gone home, got guns, and shot back.

We knew nothing about this at the time and went home. In the morning someone came around and told us they'd heard we got shot. I said, nope. When I heard who had been shot I laughed and laughed, it was the best thing that could have happened to us. Reservoir were our enemies so were the Lalor guys, we'd had trouble with them for years, we'd had a few shoot outs with them too. They've shot each other, they're all out of action, and the coppers are on their backs. We went in for the kill. We went down to belt up Reservoir, they didn't want no trouble, about four of them joined up with us. We also got control of Lalor and a lot of publicity out of it and everyone wanted to join up with us, sharps from as far as Elsternwick and Caulfield. The bad thing was the coppers were everywhere we went. We'd go to the shops to meet and within five minutes there'd be eight cop cars there. There were warnings in the local paper saying any Thomastown sharps who go into Reservoir will get pinched by the police. I thought, oh yeah, sure. So I got a few of the boys together, two carloads, got into Reservoir and they were waiting for us. The Senior Detective, Stubbs, was a real smart copper, never got violent but he'd done his homework. He lined us up in the station and he knew all our nick-names- Peewee, Tiger...

That night I got charged, my first offence. I had a meat cleaver in the car.

We had a few run-ins with Westside Sharps. At first we were alright with Westside, well some of them anyway. They were nothing to us, we were the number one gang. Then one of our guys, Murray, had a fight with one of them. I didn't want to start with Westside because I didn't mind them, but I had to go along with what the boys wanted to do. So we organised another one out between Murray and the other guy, Keith, in Footscray Park. It was a good fight! They were at it for a while, but then Keith got the better of Murray. Westside were worried we were going to jump them, so they broke it up, even though there was only twenty of us and forty of them. I wanted to leave it at that, but from then on we were enemies. We got them at the Show about six months later. Wrecked them, threw them through shop windows, most of them ran off. Years later I became friends with some of their top-boys.

One night about five carloads of Black Dragons came down and beat up some of our guys in a Lalor pizza parlour. From then on we were fighting the Black Dragons. We ran into about twelve of them at the Show one night. A few of them were supposed to be Martial Arts instructors, they formed a straight line, turned around into a Karate stance, and all jumped into the air with a front kick. It was on. One of our guys was taking photos, I'd given him the camera earlier because I wanted some action shots. The Black Dragons ran off, supposedly the first time they'd been beaten. That night we got escorted back to Thomastown by twenty railway detectives- we had blood all over us, split heads, no one said a thing, we just sat there.

Near the end we were bringing guns out because everyone else was, people wouldn't fight us no more unless they came with guns. We went and shot up Cravelli Street, a very tough street gang in Preston, they'd beat up one of our guys. We also had a few run-ins with West Heidelberg.

I was a kid when it started, but I grew out of it. I went into bouncing and did it for ten years. Same thing but I got paid for it. A lot of the guys are dead or junkies. I stopped seeing them when they got into drugs, didn't want no part of it.

The last time I went out with Thomastown Sharps was the AC/DC 'Back In Black' concert at the Myer Music Bowl. About seventy of us went that night. A lot of them were young guys, a lot of the older guys had drifted out of the scene. I was getting sick of it by then. That night we punched up Westside Sharps, after that there was a bit of a truce with them. We also fought Vic Sharps and had a big fight with the Lebanese Tigers, one of them got smashed with a stubby bottle and lost an eye."

5

THE EIGHTIES

In London, February 1980, Bon Scott's mile-a-minute lifestyle finally caught up with him- death by alcoholic misadventure. Trade Schools, roller rinks and coffee bars Melbourne wide fell into a slough of despond.

Bon's passing might easily have finished AC/DC, but they soldiered on, recruiting Brian Johnson, he of the eternal flat cap and sandpaper screech, formerly singer with British glam-heavies Geordie.

I've never really gone in for post-Bon Seedies, too much thud, not enough grind. 'Back in Black' the group's first album with Johnson is the exception, it's all thud, but it's consummate thud, and though it's not quite up there with the best of the Bon years, it's as near as no matter.

'Back in Black' was a worldwide smash. It made number two on the Australian charts and a tour was announced for '81. The band's Melbourne concert was one of the most significant moments in the great sharp epic. It was the grand finale, the last big night on the town. The cult carried on for a few more years, but it was trudging to a fall. Sharpie ended that night, it just took a while for word to get around.

Held at the Myer Music Bowl during the Moomba Celebrations, the concert was at once a wake and a whale of a party. The Seedies/The Music Bowl/ Moomba- ultimate sharpie.

The gangs came out in force. They ran amok. Gloves off.

Bill
"They were everywhere, it was like they'd all taken their clothing out of their glory boxes for the night."

Chris
"Every sharp in Melbourne would've been there, they went beserk, smashed all the trains and trams, pulled the cops off their horses, a riot. I got smacked in the mouth and ran for my life. By this stage I was into punk, the ballroom, speed, to me these kids, with the moccasins and Bon Scott RIP t-shirts, they weren't sharpies, they were just head bangers."

Sharp may have been near extinction, but there were still quite a few stragglers out there, and some neighbourhoods boasted sharpie mobs until '83/84.

The teenage world is arcane in the extreme. Any write up on teen-trends, not written by a teenager, should be taken with a huge cargo of salt. No adult really knows the score, not even those that fancy themselves experts in the field. Outer-suburban teenagers are a doubly mysterious breed. Nobody really gives a hoot what they're into. Out of sight, out of mind.

Thus it was possible for pockets of sharpie to survive all but unnoticed in some back-block hamlets, years after the cult was finished as a large scale, newsworthy phenomenon.

Sharp's glory days may have been long gone but they weren't completely forgotten. There were plenty of lads hitting their teens who remembered sharpie as the height of tearaway cool. They wanted to take on a tough-guy image and sharpie filled the bill admirably.

Maybe their older brothers had been sharps, or they'd simply grown up hearing tales of the local squad, how they'd ruled the roost and taken no shit. Or perhaps, as is often the case, one or two of the old-timers were still knocking around the teenage haunts, filling the youngsters' starstruck ears with how things used to be, the clout, the camaraderie.

These were the kids who kept the style alive in the eighties, long after it was assumed dead. There were some big mobs out there too. They'd come into town, maraud Angels' concerts,

and play their roles to the hilt. But they were like those Japanese soldiers stuck on Pacific Islands, convinced WW2 was still raging, years after everyone else had made-up mates and gone home. They were an anachronism.

Bill
"I went to a Kiss concert with some friends and we met some sharps from Dandenong, about twenty guys, never seen them before. We tried to make friends with them but they wanted a fight. I guess living out in Dandenong they didn't know what was happening, still sharpies, bumpkins."

It couldn't last. They were living on bygone glories. By 1984 the last whisper had died away and sharp was well and truly over and out.

THE END

ACKNOWLEDGEMENTS

I'd like to express my gratitude to all the ex-sharps that put me in the picture and provided me with the photos and quotations that are the backbone of the book:

Chris O'Halloran, Bill, Dennis Boyles, Virginia, Peter Wilkins, Lisa Moore, Martin Brown, Radar, Sam Biondo, Ken Hurrey, Mark the Coburg droog, Dale Hall, Julie Boyd, Cliff, Tony Dickinson, Suzanne Chalson, John Bow, Edwina, Garry Daniel, Chane Chane, Arthur and Rod- The Oakleigh Boys, Fiona Dent, Sally Hueston, Roy Christou, Bob Sandford.

Also, the Rock n' Rollers:
Lobby Loyde, Angry Anderson, Greg Macainsh, Ken Murdock, Daryl Braithwaite, Max Vella.

And:
The City Of Melbourne- Arts and Culture Branch, Iain McIntyre (without whom there wouldn't be a book), Jeremy Gronow from Leader Newspaper, Denise Hall, Sammy Barbagallo, Sarah from Mushroom, Judith Bessant, Debbie Lyde, Emily O'Connell, Eugene Docherty, Rose, Dereck Herbert from the Australian Academy Of Boxing, Laurel Smith from APRA, Jane Koetsveld, Beck, Rachel, Matt, Stew and Tim.

And most of all, Rallou and my parents, to whom this book is dedicated.

Michael Helms
FATAL VISIONS
THE WONDER YEARS
2012, LedaTape Org., 248pp

Melbourne's own infamous trash film zine has congealed into perfect bound format!

This compilation covers the earliest and rarest entries in FVs decade-long publication history. Devoted to sleaze, violence and sexploitation, bottom of the package video titles, late late night TV movies, films that played as drive-in supports and in hard tops where they were lucky to play for one week only.

Thee Rockhunter
SONIC ANTIQUARIAN
2011, LedaTape Org., 128pp

From the back alleys of pub rock to the heady myths of classical Hauntiquarianism, The Rockhunter accompanies you on a journey without a destination in a land with so many names the map's worn through by over-printing. Rock history's never made more (or less) sense. Profusely illustrated and featuring a comprehensive bibliography and index (conditions apply).

Ecclesfield ❀ Hove ❀ Collingwood ❀ Mission District
The LedaTape Organisation

 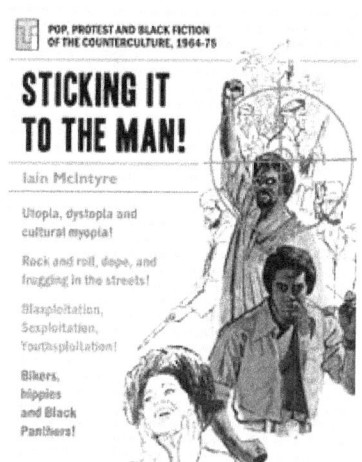

Palmer, Strong, Taylor et al.
EDGED WEAPONS!?
ALL OF THE ACTUAL FACTS ABOUT THE BEAT TANDOORI AND THE HOVE UNDERGROUND 1989 AND ALL THAT.

forthcoming, LedaTape, ~200pp

Candied photos plus anecdotes, poems, comix, shopping lists and obscene doodles from the heyday of the world's least influential "movement" that spawned countless books and records that have been mercilessly suppressed by the Reactionary Forces. With cameos by Stewart Home and Billy Childish. Hurh?

Iain McIntyre
STICKING IT TO THE MAN!
POP, PROTEST AND BLACK FICTION OF THE COUNTER-CULTURE, 1965-74

2012, LedaTape, 80pp

Rock n roll, dope and frugging in the streets! Utopia, dystopia and cultural myopia! Bikers, hippies and Black Panthers! Over 120 covers and reviews of fictional novels drawing upon the political and social upheaval of the counterculture era. Dig in to discover a lost world of of mind-bending militants, thinly veiled manifestoes and trashy exploitation.

— www.ledatape.net —
"Our shit beats your gold..."

www.ingramcontent.com/pod-product-compliance
Lightning Source LLC
Chambersburg PA
CBHW051451290426
44109CB00016B/1716